Group Work

Intermediate

Peter Watcyn-Jones

To Kirsten Woest and
Sakranchit Kanjanasoot (Oye)
with warm memories

PENGUIN ENGLISH

Pearson Education Limited
Edinburgh Gate
Harlow
Essex CM20 2JE, England
and Associated Companies throughout the world.

ISBN 978-0-582-46158-1

First published 2000
Copyright © Peter Wateyn-Jones 2000
Seventh impression 2010

Design and typesetting by Ferdinand Pageworks, London
Illustrations by Chris Rothero/Linden Artists
Printed in China   SWTC/07

Photocopying notice
The pages in this book marked From GROUP WORK INTERMEDIATE by Peter Watcyn-Jones © Penguin Books 2000 **Photocopiable** may be photocopied free of charge for classroom use by the purchasing individual or institution. This permission to copy does not extend to branches or additional schools of an institution. All other copying is subject to permission from the publisher.

Acknowledgement
'Greedyguts' (p92) from *Hot Dog and Other Poems* by Kit Wright, published by Kestrel 1981 © Kit Wright 1981.

Published by Pearson Education Limited in association with Penguin Books Ltd, both companies being subsidiaries of Pearson plc.

For a complete list of the titles available from Penguin English please write to your local Pearson Education office or to:
Marketing Department, Pearson Education, Edinburgh Gate, Harlow, Essex CM20 2JE

Contents

Introduction

Several years ago I wrote two of the first books that were entirely devoted to pair work. Shortly after writing these books I got the idea for **Group Work (Intermediate)** which is based entirely on group work. I hope teachers will find it as enjoyable to use as I have found to write.

The organisation of this book

The activities have been grouped according to types of activities. Altogether there are eight sections: *Ice-breaker activities, Simulations/role-plays, Discussion/speaking activities, Problem-solving activities, Reading/writing activities, Quizzes, Card and board games* and *Miscellaneous activities*. Part 1 of the book gives detailed Teacher's notes for each activity while Part 2 contains the various cards, handouts, etc. to be photocopied.

Where possible, the material to be photocopied has been arranged in such a way that it also serves as an instant key to the majority of the activities. For example, in the jigsaw reading activities the broken sentences are arranged on the page in the correct order. It is therefore important to remember to shuffle the cards prior to handing them out to the students. Where a key is not obvious from the layout, a separate key is included in the Teacher's notes.

Classroom organisation

Although class sizes vary considerably, the book assumes an average class size of 15–20 students. Where possible, the classroom should be physically rearranged to facilitate working in groups. However, should this not be possible, even the more traditional front-facing rows of desks can be easily adapted for group work. For example, two students can easily turn their chairs round to face two others behind them. The majority of activities in this book is for groups of four students. From experience, I have found this to be the optimum number since it allows each student to participate fully and there is less risk of some students either dominating the group or being silent and contributing very little.

The role of the teacher

Apart from one or two teacher-led activities, the teacher's role is largely that of coordinator. He or she is mainly responsible for:

- preparing the material in sufficient quantities
- explaining clearly what is to be done
- 'checking' answers at the end of an activity.

Once an activity has started, students usually work independently of the teacher at their own pace. The teacher goes round the classroom listening and monitoring their progress and only interfering or helping if *absolutely necessary*.

Time-limits

Although many teachers may disagree with me on this point, I strongly advise giving the class a time-limit for most of the activities, and to stop them whether they have finished or not. Apart from the obvious difficulties of students finishing at different times, the checking process is often an integral and, from the learning point of view, important part of the activity. As such it is better that you check with the whole class rather than with individual groups.

Storing the material

The material to be photocopied can be divided into two types: (a) handouts which the students write on, and (b) material which the students use but do not write on.

To save the teacher unnecessary work, therefore, it is a good idea that the material to be re-used is made as durable as possible. One way is to mount everything on thin card. (Many photocopiers nowadays allow the use of card.) These cards and handouts can then be stored in separate envelopes (clearly labelled on the outside) which can be handed back to the teacher at the end of the activity.

All of the activities presented in this book require preparation on the part of the teacher. It is hoped that all the extra effort will prove to be rewarding.

Part 1: **Teacher's notes**

Ice-breaker activities

These activities are intended largely for fun – to be used with new groups to 'break the ice'.

1   Speculating

This is an ice-breaker activity where students speculate about the other people in their group. It is for groups of three to four students.

Method

1   Copy the handouts on pages 12–15 – one for each student in the group (A, B, C and D).
2   Students work alone to start with. Allow 5–10 minutes for them to speculate about the other three members of the group. Tell them that they can only write one name in each space. They then indicate whether they think the answer is *Yes* or *No*.
3   When they have finished, they take it in turns to ask the people whose names they had written on their sheet an appropriate question to see if they had guessed correctly about them. If so, they put a tick in the box marked *Correct?*
4   The student who gets the most ticks in the *Correct?* column wins.

2   Get to know your group

This is an activity based on students answering questions about themselves and their lives. It is suitable for groups of up to six students.

Method

1   Copy, cut up and shuffle the number cards on pages 16 and 17 – one set for each group. Also copy Questions: Set 1 or Questions: Set 2 on pages 18 and 19 – one copy for each group.
2   The students work in groups of four to six. Give each group a set of number cards plus a handout of the questions. Tell them to place the number cards face down on the table. The first person in the group turns up a number, looks at the equivalent question on the handout and asks someone in the group the question. That person must try and answer. (But tell them that they can always 'Pass' if they can't think of an answer or don't want to answer.)
3   The next person now picks up a number and again asks someone the appropriate question. The activity continues in this manner.
4   Set a time-limit (e.g. 20 minutes), then stop everyone. (Few groups will have had time to go through all the questions.)

Simulations/Role-plays 🎭

These activities give the students, amongst other things, a chance to try their hand at 'acting'. Often

the shyest students come to life when hiding behind a role!

3   Holiday talk

This is a simulation/role-play for four students based on talking about a recent holiday.

Method

1   Copy and cut up the handout on pages 20 and 21 – one for each student in the group (A, B, C and D).
2   Allow 5–10 minutes for the students to read through their handouts and to work out where they went on holiday, etc. The students work alone at this stage.
3   When everyone is ready, the role-play can begin. Before they start, arrange the chairs to resemble a train compartment, with pairs of students facing each other. Student C begins.
4   Set a time-limit (e.g. 15–20 minutes), then stop everyone, *whether they have finished or not.*

4   Arranging a party

This is a simulation/role-play for four people based on trying to make arrangements for an end-of-term party.

Method

1   Copy and cut up the handouts on pages 22 and 23 – one for each student in the group (A, B, C and D).
2   Allow 5–10 minutes for the students to read through their handouts. The students work alone at this stage.
3   When everyone is ready, the role-play can begin. Before they start, arrange the chairs with pairs of students facing each other. Student C begins.
4   Set a time-limit (e.g. 15–20 minutes), then stop everyone, *whether they have finished or not.*

5   At a party

This is a very simple yet effective role-play where students imagine they are extremely successful and famous people who meet other equally successful and famous people at a top London hotel.

Method

1   Copy the handout on page 24, one copy for each student.
2   Divide the class into groups of up to ten people. Go through the instructions on the handout with the whole class, so that the students fully understand what they have to do. Also draw their attention to the list of useful phrases that they can use when talking to people. Allow approximately 5–8 minutes for them to prepare their roles.
3   Allocate classroom space for each group and let the role-play begin. (The teacher can go from

group to group, pretending to be a waiter and offering drinks, small snacks, etc. – mimed of course!)

4   Set a time-limit (e.g. 15–20 minutes), then ask one or two students to introduce some people they met and to tell the rest of the class one or two things about them.

6   TV programme planners

This is a simulation for groups of four to five students based on choosing the types of programmes suitable for an evening's viewing.

Method
1   Copy the handout on page 25 – one for each group. Also copy the Programme selections on page 26 – one set for each group.
2   Allow approximately five minutes for the students to read through the instructions. Make sure they all understand what they have to do.
3   When everyone is ready, the simulation can begin. Suggest that one person in the group is given the job of writing the choices on the TV planning sheet.
4   Set a time-limit (e.g. 15 minutes), then stop everyone.
5   Students now get together with another group to compare their choices.
6   Get one or two groups to read out their choices. Also check the follow-up question, namely: *What would your 'perfect' TV evening be?*

7   Luxury cruise

This simulation/role-play is for four students and is based on people meeting for the first time at dinner on a luxury cruise ship.

Method
1   Copy and cut up the handouts on pages 27 and 28 – one for each student in the group (A, B, C and D).
2   Allow 5–10 minutes for the students to read through their handouts and to work out their roles. The students work alone at this stage.
3   When everyone is ready, the role-play can begin. Before they start, arrange the chairs to resemble a dining table, with pairs of students facing each other. Student B begins.
4   Set a time-limit (e.g. 15–20 minutes), then stop everyone, *whether they have finished or not.*

8   Advertising a new product

This is a simulation for groups of four to five students based on advertising a new product.

Method
1   Copy the handout on page 29 – one for each student.

2   Read through the instructions with the whole class to make sure that they know exactly what they have to do. Explain that the memo is meant to be read before the meeting. Allow them 10 minutes to do this.
3   When everyone is ready, the simulation can begin. Suggest that one person in the group is the chairperson while another person is responsible for recording any decisions made.
4   Set a time-limit (e.g. 15 minutes) then stop everyone.
5   Students now get together with another group to compare their choices.
6   Get one or two groups to read out their choices.

9   Interviewing a pop group

This is a role-play for five to six students based on journalists interviewing a new British pop group called *The Strawberries* on their first major tour of the USA.

Method
1   Copy the handouts on pages 30 and 31. (The handout for the group members is on page 30 and the handout for the journalists is on page 31.)
2   Divide the class into groups of up to six people. Three people are group members while the remaining people are journalists. Give out the appropriate handouts and make sure they read through them carefully. Allow approximately 10–15 minutes for them to prepare their roles.
3   Allocate classroom space for each group and let the role-play begin.
4   Set a time-limit (e.g. 15–20 minutes), then stop everyone.
5   For homework, the students could write a newspaper report based on the interview. The heading could be:

THE STRAWBERRIES – THE CREAM OF BRITISH POP

10 The front page

This is a simulation for groups of four to five students based on deciding the content of a daily newspaper's front page.

Method
1   Copy the handout on page 32 – one for each group. Also copy the newspaper stories and the photographs on pages 33 and 34 – one set for each group.
2   Read through the instructions with the whole class to make sure that they know exactly what they have to do.
3   Hand out the news stories and the photographs and let the groups try to work out which ones to use.

4 Set a time-limit (e.g. 15–20 minutes), then stop everyone.

5 Get each group to read out their choices for the front page of the newspaper. What was the most popular 'main' story with the groups? Which stories were the least popular?

Discussion/Speaking activities

These activities encourage the students to discuss various subjects and to agree and disagree with each other. They also give the students a chance to put forward their views or opinions about different things.

11 The invention game

This is a balloon debate with a difference, where the students imagine they are an invention rather than a person. It can be used with up to six students.

Method

1 Copy and cut up the handouts on pages 35–37 – one for each student (A–F). For groups of less than six students, choose the four most appropriate ones.

2 The students work alone to prepare their arguments.

3 When everyone is ready, they can begin. One student starts and tries to say why s/he is an invention that society cannot do without.

4 The other students continue, in turn. Finally, there can be an open debate where each person tries to think up more arguments, persuade the others, etc.

5 Set a definite time-limit (e.g. 15–20 minutes). Then each student votes for which invention to get rid of (based on the arguments s/he has heard). They are naturally **not** allowed to vote for themselves!

12 In my opinion …

This is a discussion activity for groups of three to five students, where students give their opinions on various topics and agree or disagree with each other.

Method

1 Copy and cut out the number cards* on page 38 – one set for each student and the opinion cards on page 39 – one set for each group.

2 The opinion cards are shuffled and placed face down on the table. The first student turns up a card and reads out the statement. Each person now shows his/her opinion by placing an appropriate number card in front of him/her. Before the groups begin you should explain what the numbers stand for: +1, +2 = you agree, –1, –2 = you disagree, 0 = you are undecided.

3 The first student now gives his/her opinion. After this the rest of the group can join in. Encourage them, in particular, to concentrate on students whose opinions are different or those who are, as yet, undecided. Also explain that if they change their opinion during the discussion, they show this by changing the number card in front of them. For example, a student might have placed 0 at the start, showing s/he is undecided. Then during the course of the discussion s/he starts to agree with the statement, so exchanges the '0' card for the '+1' card or the '+2' card. Tell them to spend approximately 3–5 minutes on each statement.

4 The second student now turns up a card and the whole thing begins again.

5 Set a time-limit for the activity (e.g. 20 minutes), then stop the students and have a general class discussion. (Ask groups to select the statement that caused the greatest argument.)

(*To save paper, four sets of number cards are included on the same page.)

13 What if …?

This is a discussion activity for groups of four to six students, where students speculate about things that are both possible and impossible.

Method

1 Copy, cut up and shuffle the cards on pages 40–42 – one set for each group. The groups will also need sheets of paper to write on.

2 One student in the group turns over the top card and reads it out, e.g. *If you could change one thing about yourself, what would it be?*

3 Each student now has about two minutes to write down a suitable answer. At the end of the time, each student reads out what they have written. Encourage the students to discuss the subject further if possible – especially if the answers are very different.

3 Set a time-limit (e.g. 20–25 minutes), then stop everyone.

4 Ask each group to say which card they found the most interesting to speculate about.

14 What to look for in a job

This is a discussion activity for groups of three students, based on reaching a consensus on what are the most important things to look for when choosing a job.

Method

1 Copy the handout on page 43 – one for each student.

2 Divide the class into groups of three. Give each group copies of the handout and read through the instructions with the whole class to make

sure they know what to do. At this stage you can also read through the 15 points to check they understand all the vocabulary.

3 Set a time-limit (e.g. 10–15 minutes), then stop everyone, *whether they have finished or not*. Students now find another group or groups in the class and compare and discuss their answers.

4 Ask each group to say which three items they thought were the most important. Were the groups very different or did one or two things seem common to all? Finally, ask if there was anything left out which some groups thought important.

15 Future questionnaire

This is a discussion activity for groups of three to five students, based on a questionnaire about the future.

Method

1 Copy and cut up the ABC cards on page 44 – one set of A, B, C for each student. Also copy and cut up the cards on pages 45 and 46 – one set for each group.

2 Divide the class into groups. Give each group a set of question cards which are shuffled and placed face down on the table in front of them. Also give each student a set of ABC cards.

3 One student starts by picking up the top card and reading it out with the three choices – A, B and C. (It can be read out more than once, if necessary.) Now every person lays down a card (A, B or C) to indicate their opinion. They then have a discussion about the topic on the card.

4 Set a time-limit (e.g. 15–20 minutes), then stop everyone, *whether they have gone through all the cards or not*.

5 Ask each group to say which topic they thought gave the most discussion.

Problem-solving activities

These are activities where students have to solve problems of various kinds, especially logic problems.

16 At the zoo

This is a problem-solving activity for groups of four students, where students use clues to work out where the various animals are in the zoo, in particular which building is the Seal Enclosure.

Method

1 Copy and cut out the plan of the zoo on page 47 – one for each group. Also copy and cut up the clue cards on page 47 – one for each person in the group (A, B, C and D).

2 The students work together to try to work out where the various animals are kept in the zoo in order to find out which building is the Seal Enclosure. One person acts as the group leader and is responsible for filling in the names of the various houses/enclosures (1–8). Tell the groups that they are allowed to read out their clues, but they are not allowed to write anything down or show them to each other. (The leader can only write the names of the animal houses/enclosures in the correct places – nothing else!)

3 Set a time-limit (e.g. 15 minutes), then stop everyone, *whether they have finished or not*.

4 Check orally.

Key

The buildings are as follows:

1 Lion House, 2 Gorilla House, 3 Monkey House, 4 Elephant House, 5 Giraffe House, 6 Reptile House, 7 Seal Enclosure, 8 Polar Bear Enclosure

17 What's in a job?

This is a problem-solving activity for groups of up to six students, in which they have to guess what criteria others have used in putting ten jobs in order of importance.

Method

1 Copy and cut up the cards on page 48 – one for each person in the group (A, B, C, D, E and F).

2 The students work alone at first and order their jobs according to the criteria on their card. They write their answers on a separate piece of paper. Make sure they don't let anyone else in the group see their card.

3 Students now take it in turns to read out their order. When they have finished, the others try to guess what the order was based on.

18 Two situations

This is a problem-solving activity for groups of three to four students, in which they are given two situations to discuss and decide about.

Method

1 Copy and cut up the two situations on page 49 – one for each group.

2 Give out situation 1 first. Read through it with the whole class, then let the students work out their answers. They have 15 minutes. Check orally.

3 Do the same with situation 2.

19 Pets and their owners

This is a problem-solving activity for groups of four students, in which they use clues to work out who owns which pet in a pet competition.

Method

1 Copy and cut up clue cards and tables on page 50 – one for each person in the group (A, B, C and D).

2 The students work together to try to work out which person owns which pet. The position each pet came in the competition has already been filled in. Tell the groups that they are allowed to read out their clues, but they are not allowed to show them to each other, or write anything down, apart from writing the names of the people and pets in the correct places.

3 Set a time-limit (e.g. 10–15 minutes), then stop everyone, *whether they have finished or not.*

4 Check orally.

Key

name	pet	position
Harry	parrot	1st
Julia	hamster	2nd
Amanda	cat	3rd
Jack	dog	4th
Sally	tortoise	5th

20 What clothes did they buy?

This is a problem-solving activity for groups of four students, in which they use clues to work out which articles of clothing each man bought and in which colour.

Method

1 Copy and cut up the clue cards and tables on page 51 – one for each person in the group (A, B, C and D).

2 The students work together to try to work out which article of clothing each person bought and in what colour. The names of the five men have already been filled in. Tell the groups that they are allowed to read out their clues, but they are not allowed to show them to each other or write anything down, apart from writing the names of the articles of clothing people bought and the colours.

3 Set a time-limit (e.g. 10–15 minutes), then stop everyone, *whether they have finished or not.*

4 Check orally.

Key

name	bought	colour
Peter	a jumper	black
Mark	a shirt	blue
Tom	a pair of shoes	brown
Bill	a tie	yellow
Chris	a pair of trousers	green

Reading/Writing activities

Here, all the activities involve the students reading or writing.

21 Situations from dialogues

This is both a reading and a writing activity for four students, in which they try to expand a given dialogue.

Method

1 Copy the handouts on pages 52–55 – one for each student. There are four altogether, so you can choose different ones for different groups.

2 The students work together to write six to eight extra lines both before and after the given extract.

3 Set a time-limit (e.g. 20–25 minutes), then stop everyone, *whether they have finished or not.* They now practise reading their 'extended' dialogues.

4 Ask one or more of the groups to perform their dialogue in front of the class.

22 Jigsaw reading 1

This is a useful reading activity, where the groups try to sort out a story. (There are three different ones to choose from.)

Method

1 Choose one of the stories from pages 56–58. Then copy it, cut it out and shuffle the pieces – one set for each group. Divide the class into groups of three to four students. Give each group a set of cards and tell them to arrange them in the correct order.

2 Set a definite time-limit (e.g. 15 minutes) and stop the students at the end of it, *whether they have finished or not.*

3 Check orally by getting one person from one of their groups to read the first line of the story, then another person to read the second line, and so on.

4 Get the groups to suggest a title for the story.

Key

The stories are already arranged in the correct order in the book.

23 Jigsaw reading 2

This is a useful listening and communicative activity, where the groups try to sort out a story orally, then solve a problem. (There are three different stories to choose from.)

Method

1 Choose one of the stories from pages 59–61. Then copy, cut out and shuffle it – one set for each group. Divide the class into groups of 5–8

students. Give each student one or more parts of the story. Tell them they are not allowed to let anyone else see their card(s).

2   Explain that they are allowed to read out what is on their card but they mustn't write anything down or show the cards to other members of the group. The aim is to sort out the story orally in the correct order.

3   Set a definite time-limit (e.g. 10–15 minutes) and stop the students at the end of it, *whether they have finished or not.*

4   Check orally using one of the groups. They read their story out loud in the correct order, then suggest a solution to the question posed at the end.

Acknowledgement: I was first introduced to this type of activity by Mario Rinvolucri on one of his many visits to Sweden.

Key

The stories are already arranged in the correct order in the book. The (suggested) solutions to the problems are as follows:

1   *Plane crash!*
    Neither place. You cannot bury survivors since they are still alive!

2   *Motorbike test*
    He stepped out in front of the wrong motorbike.

3   *Day trip to the seaside*
    He was in Barmouth spending a 2-week holiday there with his wife and children/girlfriend.

24 Letters to an advice column

This is a group reading/writing/discussion activity based on replies given to letters sent to the problem page of a magazine.

Method

1   Copy the handouts on page 62 – one for each student.

2   Divide the class into groups of three to four. Read through the instructions with the whole class to make sure they know exactly what they have to do. Tell them to spend about 5–6 minutes on each letter. One person in each group can be responsible for writing down the group's conclusions.

3   After 20–25 minutes stop everyone, *whether they have finished or not.*

4   Check orally, one letter at a time, by asking groups at random to read out their conclusions.

5   For homework, get the students to choose one of the replies and to write their version of the 'original' letter that was sent in to the magazine.

25 An interview

This is a writing activity for groups of three, where

the students have to work out the questions in an interview. (They know what the answers were.)

Method

1   Copy the handout on page 63 – one for each group.

2   Explain that they have fifteen answers to an interview with someone. The aim is to work out what they think the questions were. Set a time-limit (e.g. 15–20 minutes).

3   When they have finished, tell them to find another group and to compare their answers.

4   Finally, ask one or two of the groups to read out their dialogue. One person can read the answers, while the other two in the group can ask alternate questions.

5   For homework, the students could write a newspaper article based on the interview. A possible title:

FAMOUS ACTRESS THREATENS TO SUE NEWSPAPER FOR LIBEL!

Quizzes   Q

All the activities in this section are based on various types of quizzes. They are largely for fun and can often be used as end of term/course activities.

26 UK quiz

This is a quiz for teams of three to four students competing against each other. It is based on their knowledge of the UK.

Method

1   Copy the handouts on pages 64 and 65 – one set for each group.

2   Each group appoints a group leader and decides on a name for itself. The group leader is responsible for doing all the writing.

3   Each group works through the quiz. Encourage the students to guess if they don't know the answers! Allow 25–30 minutes, then stop everyone, *whether they have finished or not.*

4   Groups exchange quiz papers. Check orally with the whole class.

5   The papers are handed back. The group with the highest score is the winner.

Key

1   (c) Between 50–60 million (1 point)

2   (a) The monarch/the Queen; (b) The Prime Minister
    (1 point for each correct answer = 2 points total)

3   (a) Edinburgh; (b) Cardiff; (c) Belfast
    (1 point for each correct answer = 3 points total)

4   1 c; 2 g; 3 e; 4 a; 5 f; 6 h; 7 b; 8 d

(1 point for each correct answer = 8 points total)

5   (a) Labour Party (b) Conservative Party (or vice-versa)

    (1 point for each correct answer = 2 points total)

6   (c) Birmingham (1 point)

7   (b) Stratford-upon-Avon (1 point)

8   (a) 17; (b) 18; (c) 16; (d) 18; (e) 16

    (1 point for each correct answer = 5 points total)

9   No (1 point)

10 1 d; 2 f; 3 g; 4 e; 5 b; 6 h; 7 c; 8 a

    (1 point for each correct answer = 8 points total)

11 Choose from the following:

    The Times, The Guardian, The Independent, The Daily Telegraph, The Sun, The Daily Mirror, The Daily Express, The Daily Mail, The Daily Sport, The Daily Star

    (1 point for each correct answer = 2 points total)

12 **A** Ben Nevis; **B** Glasgow; **C** Belfast; **D** Wales; **E** Cardiff; **F** Birmingham; **G** River Thames; **H** London; **I** Oxford; **J** Isle of Wight

    (1 point for each correct answer = 10 points total)

The highest score possible for this quiz is 44.

27 An alternative quiz

This is a teacher-led quiz for teams of three to four students, but unlike other quizzes, the students are not expected to know the 'correct' answers to a question. Instead, they have to guess the most popular answer to a question (assuming that 100 people have been asked the same question). There are two sets of questions, one easier than the other. Choose the one most suitable for your class.

Method

1   Divide the class into teams of three to four. Copy the answer sheet on page 66 and cut it up – one per group. Get each team to appoint a team leader who will be responsible for recording the team's answers. Also tell each team to make up a name for themselves and to write this at the top of the answer sheet.

2   Explain that you are going to read out twenty questions but that you are not looking for the 'correct' answer. A hundred different people have been asked these questions and the students have to decide what the *most popular answer* for each question was. (Make sure they understand this!) Here is an example question you can ask to explain what you mean:

    Q: Name a famous monster from films or TV.

    Get suggestions as to what they think most people said, then tell them that the *most popular* answer was, in fact, **King Kong**. So if they answered King Kong they would score 1 point. If they answered with any other monster (e.g. Dracula, Frankenstein) they would get nothing.

It is only if they can guess the *most popular answer* that they score points!

3   Read out the statements on the Teacher's sheet on pages 67 or 68 one at a time. Allow 1–2 minutes for the teams to write down their answers.

4   When everyone has finished, get the groups to exchange papers while you go through the answers orally. Award one point for each correct answer.

5   The team with the highest score at the end wins.

28 True or false?

This is a quiz-like activity for groups of five to seven students. They form two teams that compete against each other, with one student being the referee and asking the questions. It is based on guessing correctly (and placing bets) as to whether certain trivia facts are true or false.

Method

1   Copy and cut out the Betting slips and True–False signs on page 69 – one for each team (two per group). Also copy the Questions on pages 70 and 71 for the referee in each group and the score card on page 72.

2   Divide the class into groups. Each group will consist of two teams, A and B (with two or three students per team) and one referee. Each team has betting slips (10–100 points) plus a True and a False card.

3   The teams sit facing each other, with the referee at the end of the table between them.

4   Quickly demonstrate with the whole class to make sure that everyone knows what they have to do. Say the following:

    Nobody has a key to Number 10 Downing Street, the official residence of the British Prime Minister. The door only opens from the inside.

    Now ask each group to decide whether the above is *True* or *False*. In addition, get them to place bets on their answer. They can bet between 10–100 points. If they are correct, they gain the points. If they are wrong, they lose them.

    Answer: *True*

5   Team A start. The referee asks them to choose a number between 1–40 (e.g. 15). The referee looks at question 15 and reads it out loud. Then each team decides if they think it is true or false and how much they are prepared to bet on their answer. The referee says: *Give your answer now*, whereupon each team places their *True* or *False* card on the table, plus their bet (10–100 points). The referee writes down the bets on the score sheet. S/he now reads out the answer and makes adjustments to the scores. If correct, the score is added to the total. If wrong, it is deducted. Each group starts with 1,000 points

and at the end of each round, the referee reads out the new totals, e.g. if Team A had bet 20 points and got it wrong and Team B had bet 80 and got it right, then at the end of round 1, Team A would have 980 points and Team B 1080 points.

6   It is now Team B's turn to ask for a question. Again each team says whether they think it is true or false and places their bets. The referee should keep note of the questions asked as the same question cannot be asked twice.

7   After ten questions, the game stops. The team with the highest score at the end wins.

8   If there is time, the game can be played again, with someone else being referee. Since there are 40 questions altogether, it can be played four times without reusing any questions.

29 Vocabulary quiz

This is another teacher-led quiz. It is a vocabulary quiz for teams of three to four students competing against each other.

Method

1   Copy the answer sheet on page 73 – one for each group.

2   Each group appoints a group leader and decides on a name for itself. The group leader is responsible for doing all the writing.

3   The teacher reads out the questions on pages 74 and 75 one at a time. Allow 1–2 minutes for the groups to record their answers. Do *not* read out the answers at this stage.

4   Groups exchange quiz papers. Check orally with the whole class by reading through the questions again and reading out the answers (or asking the groups to suggest them). Award points and read out any extra information on the teacher's sheet.

5   The papers are handed back. The group with the highest score is the winner.

Card and board games

These activities involve the use of cards and boards.

30 Explain the words

This is a board game for four students based on trying to explain the meaning of a word in context, and by doing so, scoring points. You will also need dice (one for each group) and counters (one for each player).

Method

1   Copy and cut up the handout on page 76 – one for each group. Give each group a dice. Each player will also need a counter (e.g. a coin, button, etc.)

2   Students decide who will be A, B, C and D, then place their counters on the appropriate starting place.

3   Student A starts. S/he throws the dice, then moves along the board that number of squares. Explain that you are allowed to move in any direction, both horizontally and vertically, even in the same turn. (In this way, it should be possible to easily reach any square on the board.)

4   Student A now tries to explain the meaning of the word **in bold type** in that square. If the rest of the group agree with his/her explanation, that square is crossed out and Student A gains the number of points shown there. If the group disagree or if Student A is unable to explain the word, then the square is not crossed out and no points are scored. If the group cannot agree whether an explanation is correct or not, the teacher is called in to adjudicate.

5   Student B now throws the dice. Play continues as before.

6   If a student ends up on a square that is crossed out, he/she misses that turn. (More likely towards the end of the game as more and more words are used up.)

7   Set a time-limit (e.g. 15–20 minutes), then stop everyone. The player with the highest score wins.

31 Ask the right question

This is a card game for three to four, where one student has the answer to a question (a hidden word) and, by asking the rest of the group questions, tries to get someone to work out what the hidden word is.

Method

1   Copy and cut up the cards on page 77 – one set for each group.

2   The cards are shuffled and placed face down on the table.

3   One student starts. S/he picks up a card and tries to ask a question that will make someone answer with this word. The person who answers first keeps the card and gains 1 point.

4   It is now the next person's turn. S/he picks up the next card and the game continues as before.

5   Set a definite time-limit (e.g. 15 minutes). The student with the highest number of points at the end is the winner.

Note

If a student has asked several questions and no one has answered correctly, then rather than go on for ever, tell the student to give the answer. Naturally, if this happens, no one scores any points.

32 Carry on the story

This is a card game for three to four students in which they have to make up a story using set words on cards.

Method

1 Copy and cut up the cards on page 78 – one set for each group.
2 The words are shuffled and each group member is dealt ten cards. (They can look at them, but tell them not to show the others in the group.)
3 One student starts. S/he begins a story. It can be about anything, but each person is only allowed to say one sentence. The aim is to include one or more of the words in his/her hand into this sentence. If s/he succeeds, the card or cards are placed face up on the table in front of him/her.
4 It is now the next person's turn. Again, s/he makes up a sentence to continue the story, trying to use up one or more of his/her words.
5 The story continues until someone gets rid of all his/her cards.

Note

Since this is meant to be a story, students can challenge someone if they think his/her sentence doesn't really make sense as far as the story is concerned.

33 Three-in-a-row: What's the question?

This is a board game for two teams (three students per team), where teams try to work out the correct questions to given answers. If correct, they capture squares on the board. The aim is to be the first team to get 'three-in-a-row'.

Method

1 Copy the board on page 79 – one for each group. Also copy and cut up the cards on pages 80–82 – one set for each group.
2 Demonstrate first by giving the class the following answer and then asking them to suggest the exact question that was asked. (NOTE: It has to be the *exact* question, so make sure this is clear before they start.)

Answer: *It's a type of weapon.*
Question: *What's a gun?*

3 The students now work in their groups. They sit facing each other with the board between them and the cards face down on the table. Team A starts. They choose a square (e.g. 10). Team B now picks up the top card from the pack and reads out the answer. Team A now have one minute to try to guess the correct answer. Team B can only say yes or no. If they guess correctly, they mark the letter A in that square. If

incorrect, the card is placed at the bottom of the pack and can be asked again later.
4 Team B now choose a square and play continues as above. The game goes on until one team has gained three squares in a row – either vertically or horizontally.

34 The category game

This is a card game for three teams (two students per team), where teams try to think of five things related to a certain category, e.g. five things you can eat, five words to do with the weather, etc.

Method

1 Copy and cut up the cards on pages 83–85 – one set for each group. Also copy the answer sheet on page 86 – one copy for each team.
2 The cards are shuffled and placed face down on the table in front of the teams. The top card is turned up, e.g. *Name five adjectives to describe people*. Each team now has 2 minutes to record their answers. Everyone then stops writing and they read out what they have written in turn. They score 1 point for every answer that is unique i.e. that no one else has written down. They write down their total score for Round 1.
3 The next card is now turned up and again they record their answers.
4 Play continues in this manner until ten cards have been turned up.
5 The points for each round are now added up and the team with the highest score at the end are the winners.

Miscellaneous activities

The remaining activities in the book do not fit into any of the previous categories.

35 Half a crossword

In this activity the students work in two groups of two to four. One group is called A and the other B. Each group has an incomplete crossword. By asking for and giving definitions, they try to fill in the missing words. (The words here are all adjectives to describe moods, states and feelings.)

Method

1 Copy the crosswords on page 87 (Group A) and page 88 (Group B).
2 Divide the class into A and B groups of between two and four students per group. They sit facing each other. Give each group the appropriate crossword and allow them time to check through the words they will need to define before starting. If necessary, give individual help

at this stage. (NOTE: On no account must they allow the other group to see their crossword.)

3   Explain that they have to take it in turns to ask for a word that is missing from their crossword. They simply ask: *What's 3 down? What's 14 across?* etc. The other group now try to give as clear a definition as possible to help them guess the word.

4   Set a definite time-limit (e.g. 20 minutes) and stop the students at the end of it, *whether they have finished or not.*

5   They can now compare crosswords and check any words they didn't fill in.

6   You can follow up by asking the groups to explain how they defined one or two words from the crossword.

36   Complete the drawing

This is a drawing/memory activity for groups of five or six students.

Method

1   Make one copy of the master sheet on page 89. Also make one copy per group of the group sheet on page 90.

2   Divide the class into groups. Tell each group to allocate one person to do the drawing for the group. Hand out a group sheet to each group. Explain that the drawing is incomplete, and that by working together they are going to try to complete it.

3   The class all work at the same time. The teacher places the master drawing on his/her desk, with its back to the class. (You can mount it like a photograph.)

4   One person from each group now comes out to the front and is allowed to look at the master drawing for 1 minute. Then they go back to their groups and *without touching anything themselves* tell the person who is doing the drawing what to draw. (They obviously won't remember every detail.)

5   Let a few minutes pass, then get the next person in the group out. Again, they look at the master drawing for 1 minute, then go back to their respective groups.

6   The activity continues until every student in the group has been out to the front. Finally, the person doing the drawing comes out for a final look.

7   The teacher now goes to each group in turn to see how well they have done. Award them a mark out of 10.

Note

You could also make extra copies of the master sheet and hand these out to the group at the end for them to see how closely their drawing resembled the original.

37   The trivia game

This is a light-hearted game for groups of three to four students, based on trying to guess the missing words in 'trivia' facts.

Method

1   Copy the handout on page 91 – one copy for each group.

2   Tell the groups that they have to try to guess what the missing words are in each of the sentences on the handout.

3   Set a time-limit (e.g. 15–20 minutes), then stop everyone, *whether they have finished or not.*

4   Check orally.

Key

1 5,000 and 6,000   **2** coughing   **3** 10%   **4** their own names   **5** seven   **6** Mohammed/Muhammad   **7** Denmark   **8** river   **9** 233   **10** jump   **11** 20   **12** cats **13** port   **14** high heels   **15** coffee   **16** the; I   **17** sticking the tongue out   **18** Iceland   **19** speaking in front of a crowd/public speaking   **20** 27

38   Choral reading

Choral reading is very useful for practising reading, pronunciation and intonation. This activity concentrates on a humorous poem with mimed actions. The students can work in groups of up to six students.

Method

1   Copy the poem on page 92 – one copy for each student.

2   Divide the class into groups (maximum six students) and give out the poems. Go through it with the whole class first, explaining any necessary vocabulary.

3   Get one person from each group to be the group leader. S/he will 'conduct' the others in the reading of the poem. Set a time-limit for rehearsal (e.g. 10–15 minutes). The group decides who will read the two solo parts. Encourage the groups to mime the actions in the poem as they read them, especially the two soloists.

4   Let each group perform the poem in front of the class.

Acknowledgement: The poem is taken from *Hot Dog and Other Poems* by Kit Wright, published by Puffin Books 1982.

Part 2:
Material for photocopying

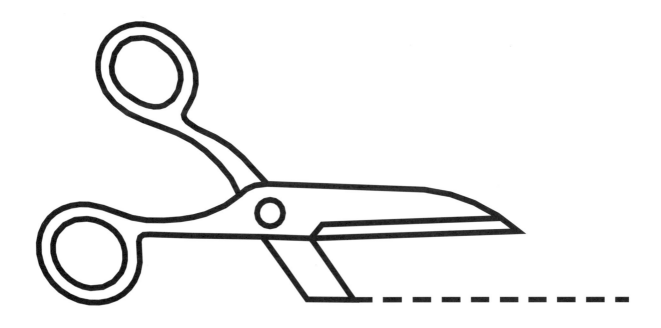

 **1 Speculating**

Work alone. See how much you know (or can guess) about the others in your group. Look at the ten sentences below. Complete each one by filling in the name of someone in your group. Try to use the names of each person at least twice.

I think ...

		Yes	No	Correct?
1	.... prefers tea to coffee.	☐	☐	☐
2	.... has used the Internet.	☐	☐	☐
3	.... loves children.	☐	☐	☐
4	.... has never eaten Indian or Chinese food.	☐	☐	☐
5	.... thinks he/she is strong.	☐	☐	☐
6	.... was born in January, February or March.	☐	☐	☐
7	.... had a shower this morning.	☐	☐	☐
8	.... always has a party on his/her birthday.	☐	☐	☐
9	.... can knit.	☐	☐	☐
10	.... is afraid of heights.	☐	☐	☐

When you have finished, take it in turns to see how 'right' you were by asking the various people questions. For example:

- Do you prefer tea to coffee (*Kurt*)?
- Do you love children (*Mario*)?
- Did you have a shower this morning (*Eva*)?
  etc.

If you guess correctly, put a tick (✔) in the box marked *Correct?*

When you have all finished, see who got the most correct guesses.

Photocopiable   From *Group Work (Intermediate)* by Peter Watcyn-Jones © Penguin Books 2000

Work alone. See how much you know (or can guess) about the others in your group. Look at the ten sentences below. Complete each one by filling in the name of someone in your group. Try to use the names of each person at least twice.

I think ...

		Yes	No	Correct?
1	.... thinks he/she is shy.	☐	☐	☐
2	.... can spell his/her name backwards in English.	☐	☐	☐
3	.... doesn't like opera.	☐	☐	☐
4	.... enjoys flying.	☐	☐	☐
5	.... usually gets up before 7.30 in the morning.	☐	☐	☐
6	.... goes dancing at weekends.	☐	☐	☐
7	.... prefers cats to dogs.	☐	☐	☐
8	.... is a good swimmer.	☐	☐	☐
9	.... watches at least two hours TV every day.	☐	☐	☐
10	.... can play the piano or the guitar.	☐	☐	☐

When you have finished, take it in turns to see how 'right' you were by asking the various people questions. For example:

- Do you like opera (*Kurt*)?
- Are you a good swimmer (*Mario*)?
- Can you play the piano or the guitar (*Eva*)?
  etc.

If you guess correctly, put a tick (✔) in the box marked *Correct?*

When you have all finished, see who got the most correct guesses.

 **1 Speculating**

Work alone. See how much you know (or can guess) about the others in your group. Look at the ten sentences below. Complete each one by filling in the name of someone in your group. Try to use the names of each person at least twice.

I think ...

		Yes	No	Correct?
1	.... believes in astrology.	☐	☐	☐
2	.... usually goes to bed after 11 o'clock at night.	☐	☐	☐
3	.... can tell a joke in English.	☐	☐	☐
4	.... is afraid of mice.	☐	☐	☐
5	.... 's favourite colour is blue or red.	☐	☐	☐
6	.... has never smoked.	☐	☐	☐
7	.... is a good dancer.	☐	☐	☐
8	.... likes to sing in the bath or shower.	☐	☐	☐
9	.... was born in the summer.	☐	☐	☐
10	.... doesn't like dogs.	☐	☐	☐

When you have finished, take it in turns to see how 'right' you were by asking the various people questions. For example:

- Do you believe in astrology (*Kurt*)?
- Are you afraid of mice (*Mario*)?
- Were you born in the summer (*Eva*)?
  etc.

If you guess correctly, put a tick (✔) in the box marked *Correct?*

When you have all finished, see who got the most correct guesses.

Photocopiable *From Group Work (Intermediate)* by Peter Watcyn-Jones © Penguin Books 2000

Work alone. See how much you know (or can guess) about the others in your group. Look at the ten sentences below. Complete each one by filling in the name of someone in your group. Try to use the names of each person at least twice.

I think ...

		Yes	No	Correct?
1 .... is interested in politics.		☐	☐	☐
2 .... believes in flying saucers.		☐	☐	☐
3 .... has more than two brothers or sisters.		☐	☐	☐
4 .... would like to do a bungee jump or a parachute jump.		☐	☐	☐
5 .... was born in August, September or October.		☐	☐	☐
6 .... prefers classical music to pop music.		☐	☐	☐
7 .... washed his/her hair last night.		☐	☐	☐
8 .... often loses his/her temper.		☐	☐	☐
9 .... is the youngest person in his/her family.		☐	☐	☐
10 .... usually reads a newspaper every day.		☐	☐	☐

When you have finished, take it in turns to see how 'right' you were by asking the various people questions. For example:

- Are you interested in politics (*Kurt*)?
- Do you prefer classical music to pop music (*Mario*)?
- Are you the youngest person in your family (*Eva*)?
  etc.

If you guess correctly, put a tick (✔) in the box marked *Correct?*

When you have all finished, see who got the most correct guesses.

1	2	3	4
5	6	7	8
9	10	11	12
13	14	15	16

 From *Group Work (Intermediate)* by Peter Watcyn-Jones © Penguin Books 2000

17	18	19	20
21	22	23	24
25	26	27	28
29	30	31	32

1 Describe a good TV programme you have seen recently.

2 Describe a happy event from your childhood.

3 Describe a teacher at school you really liked.

4 Describe a teacher at school you really disliked.

5 Describe a time when you felt really embarrassed.

6 Describe one of your brothers, sisters or friends.

7 Describe someone who has made a big impression on you.

8 Describe your house or flat.

9 Describe your bedroom.

10 Describe your best friend when you were a child.

11 Describe your favourite dish and how to cook it.

12 Describe your favourite relative.

13 Describe how you think you will be in 10 years' time. (your job, married/single, etc.)

14 Give three reasons why you like or dislike the town you live in.

15 Give three reasons why your country would be a good place to visit as a tourist?

16 Give two adjectives to describe a good friend.

17 Give two adjectives to describe a good teacher.

18 How do you usually spend your free time?

19 Is it better to be single or married? Give reasons for your choice.

20 Name a book you would recommend to others. Explain why.

21 Name a job you would not like to have. Explain why.

22 Name one or two things you are quite good at.

23 Name three countries you'd be happy working and living in for a few years.

24 Name three qualities you would look for in a partner.

25 Name three things that make you happy.

26 Name three things you would like to buy or own one day.

27 Name three ways in which men and women are different.

28 Name two good points and two bad points about yourself.

29 Name two habits other people have that you find annoying.

30 Name two things you are not very good at.

31 Name two things that you are afraid of.

32 Name your favourite pop singer or band and say what makes them so special?

    From *Group Work (Intermediate)* by Peter Watcyn-Jones © Penguin Books 2000

1 Say one or two ways in which you are like your mother or father.

2 Say something about the town or village where you were born.

3 Say what you are planning to do tonight.

4 Say where you spent your last holiday and what you enjoyed most about it.

5 Summarise the plot of a film you have seen recently.

6 Walking under a ladder is considered bad luck in some countries. Name two things that are considered bad luck in your country.

7 What are the most popular tourist attractions in your country?

8 What are you going to do at the weekend?

9 What did you do last weekend?

10 What do you remember about your first day at school?

11 What do you think is the greatest invention ever, and why?

12 What do you usually do in the evenings?

13 What is the ideal age to get married (a) for a man (b) for a woman?

14 What is the nicest present you have ever received?

15 What is your idea of the perfect husband or wife?

16 What sort of clothes do you like wearing?

17 What sort of things do you find difficult to learn in English?

18 What sort of things make you angry or annoyed?

19 What sort of things make you happy?

20 What things from your country would you miss if you ever emigrated?

21 What three adjectives do you think others would use to describe you as a person?

22 What three adjectives would you use to describe yourself as a person?

23 What sort of job would you like to have?

24 What type of men or women are you most attracted to?

25 What sort of films do you like watching?

26 What's the most exciting thing that has ever happened to you?

27 What's your favourite country for a holiday? Explain why.

28 Which country would you not like to visit? Explain why?

29 Which person (still alive!) would you most like to meet and why?

30 Which person from history do you hate most and why?

31 Which person from history would you most like to have met and why?

32 Would you like to be famous? Explain why or why not.

👥 3 Holiday talk   Student A

You are in a train compartment with three other people. You have just been on holiday and are on your way home. You get into conversation with your fellow-passengers and find out that they, too, have just been on holiday.

Before you start, think about the following:

- where you went and for how long
- where you stayed
- what you did in the day/evenings
- any interesting people you met
- any interesting excursions you went on
- what the weather/food was like
- the best thing about the holiday
- one bad thing that happened
- anything else you can think of

Another student will start.

When someone talks about their holiday, encourage them by asking questions, e.g. **What was the weather like? Did you go out a lot in the evenings? Would you go back there again?** etc.

Unfortunately, when you speak you have one very annoying habit. You tend to say **Yes, I know what you mean!** whenever you agree with something someone says.

👥 3 Holiday talk   Student B

You are in a train compartment with three other people. You have just been on holiday and are on your way home. You get into conversation with your fellow-passengers and find out that they, too, have just been on holiday.

Before you start, think about the following:

- where you went and for how long
- where you stayed
- what you did in the day/evenings
- any interesting people you met
- any interesting excursions you went on
- what the weather/food was like
- the best thing about the holiday
- one bad thing that happened
- anything else you can think of

Another student will start.

When someone talks about their holiday, encourage them by asking questions, e.g. **What was the food like? Did you go on any interesting excursions? What were the local people like?** etc.

Unfortunately, your ears are still funny after the flight and you don't always hear everything, so every now and again you ask, **Sorry, what did you say?**

3 Holiday talk Student C

You are in a train compartment with three other people. You have just been on holiday and are on your way home. You get into conversation with your fellow-passengers and find out that they, too, have just been on holiday.

Before you start, think about the following:

- where you went and for how long
- where you stayed
- what you did in the day/evenings
- any interesting people you met
- any interesting excursions you went on
- what the weather/food was like
- the best thing about the holiday
- one bad thing that happened
- anything else you can think of

When someone talks about their holiday, encourage them by asking questions, e.g. **Was the hotel very modern? Did you meet many interesting people? Was there anything there worth buying?** etc.

Unfortunately, when you speak you have one very annoying habit. You tend to use the expression **It was brilliant** far too often. For example, **You should have seen the beach. It was brilliant! As for the food – it was brilliant!** etc.

When everyone is ready, you can start by saying to one of the other people :
You're looking very tanned. Been on holiday, have you?

---

3 Holiday talk Student D

You are in a train compartment with three other people. You have just been on holiday and are on your way home. You get into conversation with your fellow-passengers and find out that they, too, have just been on holiday.

Before you start, think about the following:

- where you went and for how long
- where you stayed
- what you did in the day/evenings
- any interesting people you met
- any interesting excursions you went on
- what the weather/food was like
- the best thing about the holiday
- one bad thing that happened
- anything else you can think of

Another student will start.

When someone talks about their holiday, encourage them by asking questions, e.g. **What was the weather like? Did you go out a lot in the evenings? Would you go back there again?** etc.

Unfortunately, when you speak you have one very annoying habit. You don't always wait for another person to stop speaking before you start. You tend to say **Excuse me, can I just say something** or **I've just thought of something.**

4 Arranging a party   Student A

You and three of your friends have decided to have an end-of-term party and are meeting to work out the necessary arrangements. Here are some of the things that have to be worked out:

1 Whose flat will the party be held at?
2 Who will help to get it ready (move furniture, clean it, tidy up, etc.)?
3 How many people will be invited? (Only people in the class or boyfriends, girlfriends, other students, teachers, etc?)
4 What time will the party start and finish? Which day – Friday or Saturday?
5 How much food is needed? What sort? Who will buy/make it?
6 What sort of music will you have? Who can bring CDs?
7 Any other items that need to be brought – knives, forks, plates, glasses, etc. Who can bring what?
8 Who will help tidy up after the party – move back furniture, wash up, etc?
9 Anything else you can think of.

You have a large flat. You don't really want to use it because you are afraid that something will get broken. Also your landlady lives on the bottom floor and does not like parties to go on longer than 11.30 p.m. You have lots of CDs and you are prepared to take them to the party, but you hate cooking and washing up. You would like to bring your boyfriend/girlfriend.

4 Arranging a party   Student B

You and three of your friends have decided to have an end-of-term party and are meeting to work out the necessary arrangements. Here are some of the things that have to be worked out:

1 Whose flat will the party be held at?
2 Who will help to get it ready (move furniture, clean it, tidy up, etc.)?
3 How many people will be invited? (Only people in the class or boyfriends, girlfriends, other students, teachers, etc?)
4 What time will the party start and finish? Which day – Friday or Saturday?
5 How much food is needed? What sort? Who will buy/make it?
6 What sort of music will you have? Who can bring CDs?
7 Any other items that need to be brought – knives, forks, plates, glasses, etc. Who can bring what?
8 Who will help tidy up after the party – move back furniture, wash up, etc?
9 Anything else you can think of.

You have a large penthouse flat. You don't mind using it for the party, but if you do then you would like to invite the two people you share the flat with and their boyfriends/girlfriends. In fact, you think the more people who are invited the better the party will be. You would also prefer to buy plastic spoons, knives, cups, etc. You can throw them away afterwards, so no washing up! You don't like cooking very much and would prefer to order food from a take-away restaurant – pizzas or Chinese food.

 From Group Work (Intermediate) by Peter Watcyn-Jones © Penguin Books 2000

4 Arranging a party

Student C

You and three of your friends have decided to have an end-of-term party and are meeting to work out the necessary arrangements. Here are some of the things that have to be worked out:

1 Whose flat will the party be held at?
2 Who will help to get it ready (move furniture, clean it, tidy up, etc.)?
3 How many people will be invited? (Only people in the class or boyfriends, girlfriends, other students, teachers, etc?)
4 What time will the party start and finish? Which day – Friday or Saturday?
5 How much food is needed? What sort? Who will buy/make it?

6 What sort of music will you have? Who can bring CDs?
7 Any other items that need to be brought – knives, forks, plates, glasses, etc. Who can bring what?
8 Who will help tidy up after the party – move back furniture, wash up, etc?
9 Anything else you can think of.

You have quite a large flat. You don't mind using it for the party but the only problem is that you don't have any stereo equipment for playing music. You love organizing things and tend to 'take over' a discussion and boss people about. You don't mind helping with everything but feel that the washing up, cooking, etc. should be left to the opposite sex. You would like to invite some friends and your teacher.

 # 4 Arranging a party

Student D

You and three of your friends have decided to have an end-of-term party and are meeting to work out the necessary arrangements. Here are some of the things that have to be worked out:

1 Whose flat will the party be held at?
2 Who will help to get it ready (move furniture, clean it, tidy up, etc.)?
3 How many people will be invited? (Only people in the class or boyfriends, girlfriends, other students, teachers, etc?)
4 What time will the party start and finish? Which day – Friday or Saturday?

5 How much food is needed? What sort? Who will buy/make it?
6 What sort of music will you have? Who can bring CDs?
7 Any other items that need to be brought – knives, forks, plates, glasses, etc. Who can bring what?
8 Who will help tidy up after the party – move back furniture, wash up, etc?
9 Anything else you can think of.

You have a small basement flat. You think the party should be mainly for your class. You don't want to invite too many outsiders. You also think that everyone should help equally. You are prepared to do everything except move furniture. You also think it would be better to buy food rather than make it. During the discussion, you will make notes of what everyone offers to do, plus any other decisions that are made. If other people are invited, you think there should be an equal number of males and females, if possible.

From *Group Work (Intermediate)* by Peter Watcyn-Jones © Penguin Books 2000   23

🎭 5 At a party

Imagine you could choose any identity for yourself. What name would you choose? What nationality? What job? What background? (married, single), etc.

Everyone in the class is at a party at the Ritz Hotel in London. Go around talking to and meeting as many people as possible as your 'new' identity. Remember, you can be as glamorous or as important as you like.

Before you start, make up a background for yourself. Think about the following:

1 Your name, age, nationality.
2 Your job (pop star, Prime minister, head of a multinational company, actor, nuclear physicist, hairdresser for the stars, TV personality, supermodel, photographer, film director, plastic surgeon, world famous violinist, famous detective story writer, etc.) Remember, you can choose any job!
3 Where you live (place, what sort of house, etc.).
4 Your family (married, single, divorced, etc.).
5 Why you are in London. How long you are staying.
6 Anything else you can think of.

Here are some useful phrases you can use:

When introducing yourself:	Hello. I'm ...
	Hi there! My name's ...
	I don't believe we've met. My name's ...
Introducing another person:	(X) may I introduce (Y).
	(X), I'd like you to meet (Y).
	(X), this is (Y).
When leaving to talk to someone else:	It was nice meeting you. See you later.

Talk to each person for about two minutes. Try to find out his/her job and one or two other things about him/her.

From *Group Work (Intermediate)* by Peter Watcyn-Jones © Penguin Books 2000

You are television programme planners. You are meeting to plan a typical evening's viewing. Here is your planning sheet.

Time	Type of programme
18.00	The News, Weather
18.30	
22.00	The News, Weather
22.30	
00.30	Close down

Notice that some programmes have already been decided and cannot be changed.

It is your job to decide which type of programmes to have in the spaces that are left. You have three and a half hours to fill before the 10 o'clock news and two hours before TV closes down.

Look through the different programmes you can choose from and make your selection. (Write your choices on the above sheet.)

When you have finished, get together with another group and compare your choices. How many things were the same?

Finally, what would your 'perfect' TV evening be?

🎭 6 TV programme planners

Programme selections

Films *(90 mins)*

1 A romantic comedy.
2 A war film.
3 A thriller.
4 A horror film.
5 A science-fiction film.

Documentaries *(45 mins)*

1 A documentary about lions in Africa.
2 A documentary about earthquakes.
3 A documentary about child workers in India.
4 A documentary about Manchester United football club.

Comedy series *(30 mins)*

1 A comedy series about school.
2 A comedy series about London taxi drivers.
3 A comedy series about a bad football team.
4 A comedy series set in an Old People's Home.

Sport *(1 hour)*

1 Highlights from the Davis Cup match today between the USA and Australia.
2 Highlights from some of today's top European football matches.
3 Golf – highlights from the British Open.
4 Live coverage of the European Athletics Championships from Athens.

Soap operas *(30 mins)*

1 Australian soap – *Neighbours*.
2 British soap – *Eastenders*.
3 British soap – *Coronation Street*.
4 American soap – *Melrose Place*.

Music *(30 mins)*

1 Top of the Pops. (*The latest chart hits*.)
2 Irish folk dancing.
3 Looking back: The Spice Girls.
4 Ballet.
5 Great opera tenors. Part 3: Pavarotti.

Light entertainment *(30 mins)*

1 A talk show. (*Oprah Winfrey, Jerry Springer, etc. type of show*.)
2 A quiz show.
3 The holiday programme.
4 The clothes show. (*Fashion & beauty programme*.)
5 'Fly-on-the-wall' series. (*Docu-soap featuring real people, e.g. hotel staff, firemen, etc*.)

Short programmes *(5–15 mins)*

1 Cartoon film: Tom & Jerry. (*5 mins*)
2 How to paint watercolours: Trees. (*10 mins*)
3 Training your dog: Part 2. (*15 mins*)
4 Pop video. (*5 mins*)
5 Famous British buildings: Windsor Castle. (*10 mins*)
6 Dance masterclasses. Part 3: Salsa. (*15 mins*)

From *Group Work (Intermediate)* by Peter Watcyn-Jones © Penguin Books 2000

 **7 Luxury cruise**   Student A

You are on a 2-week luxury cruise. It is your first night on board and you are sitting at dinner with three others. (You have not met them before!)

Before you start, read through the following role-card. Try to remember as much as possible, so you don't have to look at it when the role-play actually starts.

You are a famous detective story writer in your own country, but are not very well-known anywhere else in the world. You are on this cruise to get some background details for the new book you are working on – MURDER IN THE CARIBBEAN. You are a very private person and don't like to tell people too much about yourself. You prefer to find out as much as you can about them instead! You have a favourite phrase: *I'll tell you about that some other time.* You also have a slight cold and can't help sneezing from time to time.

Also think about:

- where you live (house, country?)
- if you're married, single, divorced
- anything else (hobbies, interests, etc.)

Another student will start.

 **7 Luxury cruise**   Student B

You are on a 2-week luxury cruise. It is your first night on board and you are sitting at dinner with three others. (You have not met them before!)

Before you start, read through the following role-card. Try to remember as much as possible, so you don't have to look at it when the role-play actually starts.

You are a very rich widow/widower. Your husband/wife died just over a year ago. You are on the cruise to try to find a new 'partner', so you are very interested in anyone at the table of the opposite sex! You want to know all about them – especially if they are rich. You have been all over the world and love to tell people about the places you have visited. You tend to interrupt people with: *Did I tell you about the time I was in (Egypt)? Fantastic country! Fantastic people!*

You start. You can say:

I don't think we've been introduced yet. My name is ...

Also think about:

- where you live (house, country?)
- the sort of man/woman you like (tall, dark, good dancer, etc.)
- anything else (hobbies, interests, etc.)

From *Group Work (Intermediate)* by Peter Watcyn-Jones © Penguin Books 2000   **Photocopiable**   27

 **7 Luxury cruise** Student C

You are on a 2-week luxury cruise. It is your first night on board and you are sitting at dinner with three others. (You have not met them before!)

Before you start, read through the following role-card. Try to remember as much as possible, so you don't have to look at it when the role-play actually starts.

You are head of DRUGS R US, a health shop business with over 1,000 branches throughout the USA and Europe. You had a mild heart attack six weeks ago, so are on the cruise to relax and take it easy. But you love talking about health and especially the pills and medicines your company sells. (You have a cure for everything – from colds to being overweight.) You are also a vegetarian and love to try to persuade people to give up meat. Your favourite phrase is: *How old do you think I am? Go on – guess!* (You think you look ten years younger than you really are!)

Also think about:

- where you live (house, country?)
- if you're married, single, divorced
- anything else (hobbies, interests, etc.)

Another student will start.

----

 7 Luxury cruise Student D

You are on a 2-week luxury cruise. It is your first night on board and you are sitting at dinner with three others. (You have not met them before!)

Before you start, read through the following role-card. Try to remember as much as possible, so you don't have to look at it when the role-play actually starts.

You are a famous artist in your country and hope to sell your paintings abroad. That is one reason you are on the cruise. You have brought some paintings with you and would like to get people to look at them. But you are rather rude and hate stupid people. So if someone says something you think is stupid, you tend to say: *Do you really mean that? You must be stupid!* You also have a nasty habit of clearing your throat loudly before you speak.

Also think about:

- where you live (house, country?)
- if you're married, single, divorced
- anything else (hobbies, interests, etc.)

Another student will start.

 From *Group Work (Intermediate)* by Peter Watcyn-Jones © Penguin Books 2000

8 Advertising a new product

You work for an advertising agency. You are meeting to discuss a new type of washing powder you are about to launch onto the market.

The agenda for the meeting is as follows:

AGENDA

1 Name of new product
2 Type of photographs to use in the advertising campaign
3 Five major factors to stress when advertising
4 Where to advertise
5 Any other business

Before the meeting, read through the following Brief.

BRIEF

Product: XTY 657 *(washing powder)*

Please read before the meeting.

Name
Should be short and easy to say. Possibly one which sounds like something to do with washing or whiteness, e.g. GLOW.

Photographs
Have to decide what image we're aiming for. Here are some ideas:
- photos of product – large, clear with good text.
- housewife or husband using product. Clothes whiter, etc.
- glamour aspect. Beautiful girl wearing something washed in the product. Man admires her clothes. She says 'Don't thank me – thank X.'

Any other ideas?

Major factors
We need to choose *five* of the following:
- washes whiter
- low suds

- contains a new chemical: XRT
- does not pollute water
- non-toxic, safe for children
- leaves clothes feeling softer
- special dispenser – always pours out exactly the right amount
- container can be used again – cheaper in the long run
- smells of roses
- can be used to wash suede and leather
- can also be used to wash windows and cars

Where to advertise
Should we concentrate on television or cinemas, newspapers, magazines, hoardings, the Underground, buses, trains? Any other suggestions?

Which should we start with?
Try to come up with some answers before the meeting.

J.W.

You are members of a new British pop group called *The Strawberries*. You are going to be interviewed by a group of journalists at a press conference in New York on your first American tour.

Before you start, work out some sort of background for yourself.
Here are some things to think about:

Date/year group was formed

Brief background to how the group was formed

Year/Title of first hit

Latest record

Brief history of group

Which towns you will be playing at in the USA

Future plans

You should also make up your own imaginary life history, for example:

Your name (use your own or a stage name)

Date/place of birth

Family (maybe one of your parents was a famous musician?)

Instrument/vocals

Where you met the others

Interests

Married/single etc.

When you are ready, let the reporters interview you. Before you start, write your name on a piece of paper and put it in front of you for the journalists to see. (Be prepared to use your imagination!)

You are journalists. You are going to interview a new British pop group called *The Strawberries* on their first tour of the USA. They have just landed in New York and are giving a press conference

Before you interview *The Strawberries*, work out some questions to ask. (But don't let the other journalists see them!)
Here are some you can all use:

You can also think up some 'controversial' questions to ask, for example:

How long/playing together?

When/first appear in public?

How long/playing the guitar (synthesizer)?

How many hits?

Latest hit?

Which towns/playing/this tour?

Who writes the songs?

How/get on with each other?

etc.

Is it true/arrested for drunk driving?

First boyfriend/girlfriend only 13?

Smash up hotel rooms?

Is it true/(Peter)/jealous of (Steve)?

etc.

When you are ready, take it in turns to ask questions – either address your questions generally or to one of them. (If you address your question to one of them, use that person's name first. The group will have pieces of paper in front of them with their names.) But since you are journalists, try to 'grill' them a bit!

You can start by stating your name and which newspaper, magazine, radio station or TV channel you work for, for example:

Norma Clegg	**Peter Graham**
Melody Maker	*MTV*

10 The front page

Notes for editors

You are one of the editors of the Daily News.

You are meeting with the rest of the editorial team to plan tomorrow's edition of the newspaper. Here are some things you have to decide at the meeting:

1   The main front page story.

2   Two other stories to go on the front page.

3   The headlines for all three stories.

4   The front page photograph.

5   The caption to go with this photograph.

Look through the various stories and photographs and make your choices.

Remember: the front page should get people's attention, so that they will buy the newspaper. Similarly, the photograph should be eye-catching and interesting. (But it doesn't necessarily have to be connected with the main story!)

Write your decisions here:

Main story: ....

Headline: ....

Story 2: ....

Headline: ....

Story 3: ....

Headline: ....

Main photograph: No. ....

Caption: ....

....

 From *Group Work (Intermediate)* by Peter Watcyn-Jones © Penguin Books 2000

Story 1 *(plane crash)*
There was an air crash early this morning in Italy, in which a jumbo jet crashed into the Alps. It is feared that all 350 passengers have been killed.

Possible heading:
350 DEAD

Story 2 *(safe cigarette)*
A 99% safe cigarette has just been announced by King Tobacco and ICB. It looks exactly the same as an ordinary cigarette and is made from a substance called MMT. It is hoped it will go on sale to the public by the end of the year.

Possible heading:
CIGARETTE SMOKING – SAFE AT LAST?

Story 3 *(hi-jacking)*
A Boeing 737, on its way from Madrid to London, was hi-jacked by a group of terrorists. There are 250 people on board. The terrorists are demanding the release of political prisoners and have threatened to blow up the plane if their demands are not met.

Possible heading:
PLANE HI-JACKED

Story 4 *(UFO)*
Last night a flying saucer (UFO) was seen by more than 40,000 spectators at a football match between Liverpool and Arsenal. The UFO hovered over the ground for several minutes before disappearing at great speed. Several spectators panicked and hundreds had to be treated for shock and injuries. The match was stopped for ten minutes, but later continued. Liverpool won 2–1.

Possible heading:
ARE SPACEMEN FOOTBALL FANS?

Story 5 *(nuclear accident)*
This morning there was a scare at Windrush nuclear power station in the north of England when something went wrong with one of the circuits controlling a safety device. Thousands of people were evacuated from the area, but scientists just managed to prevent an explosion in time.

Possible heading:
NEAR EXPLOSION AT NUCLEAR POWER STATION

Story 6 *(earthquake)*
There was an earthquake early this afternoon in Odawara in Japan. Thousands of people have been killed and many more made homeless. The town of Odawara, south-west of Tokyo, has been almost completely destroyed.

Possible heading:
EARTHQUAKE NEAR TOKYO – THOUSANDS DEAD

Story 7 *(President shot)*
There was an assassination attempt made last night on the French President as he arrived at a banquet in Paris. Police quickly overpowered the man, but not before he had fired a shot at the President and wounded him in the shoulder. It is thought that the man is a member of a radical right-wing group. The President was rushed to hospital, but has made a good recovery and hopes to leave later today.

Possible heading:
ASSASSINATION ATTEMPT

Story 8 *(cloned baby)*
A team of doctors in India claim to have cloned the first human baby. The team, led by Dr. Indiri Gupta, say that by the end of the year they hope to have cloned a dozen more.

Possible heading:
FIRST HUMAN CLONED

<mark>## 10 The front page</mark>   Photographs

     From *Group Work (Intermediate)* by Peter Watcyn-Jones © Penguin Books 2000

11 The invention game
Student A

Imagine machines and other inventions or discoveries could talk. Also imagine that you are all travelling in a balloon that has a small hole in it and is falling. The only thing to do to save all the inventions is to throw one overboard. But which one?

You are a computer. Try to think up convincing reasons why you should not be thrown overboard. For example:

Without me,

- you couldn't use cash point machines to get money when the banks are closed
- the transport system (railways, planes) would collapse

etc.

You will take it in turns to talk. Start by saying:

I am a computer. You can't throw me overboard because ...

When everyone has finished, you can talk again. This time, try to think up arguments why another invention that has talked isn't so useful. Remember: You want someone else to be thrown overboard!

---

11 The invention game
Student B

Imagine machines and other inventions or discoveries could talk. Also imagine that you are all travelling in a balloon that has a small hole in it and is falling. The only thing to do to save all the inventions is to throw one overboard. But which one?

You are a car. Try to think up convincing reasons why you should not be thrown overboard. For example:

Without me,

- people wouldn't be able to travel around as freely as they do now
- millions of jobs would be lost

etc.

You will take it in turns to talk. Start by saying:

I am a car. You can't throw me overboard because ...

When everyone has finished, you can talk again. This time, try to think up arguments why another invention that has talked isn't so useful. Remember: You want someone else to be thrown overboard!

From *Group Work (Intermediate)* by Peter Watcyn-Jones © Penguin Books 2000

💬 11 The invention game   Student C

Imagine machines and other inventions or discoveries could talk. Also imagine that you are all travelling in a balloon that has a small hole in it and is falling. The only thing to do to save all the inventions is to throw one overboard. But which one?

You are an aeroplane. Try to think up convincing reasons why you should not be thrown overboard. For example:

Without me,

- it would take days or weeks to go abroad
- there would be no cheap package holidays to places like Spain, Turkey and so on

etc.

You will take it in turns to talk. Start by saying:

I am an aeroplane. You can't throw me overboard because ...

When everyone has finished, you can talk again. This time, try to think up arguments why another invention that has talked isn't so useful. Remember: You want someone else to be thrown overboard!

💬 11 The invention game   Student D

Imagine machines and other inventions or discoveries could talk. Also imagine that you are all travelling in a balloon that has a small hole in it and is falling. The only thing to do to save all the inventions is to throw one overboard. But which one?

You are penicillin. Try to think up convincing reasons why you should not be thrown overboard. For example:

Without me,

- many diseases and illnesses would be incurable
- the average lifespan of most people would probably only be about 40

etc.

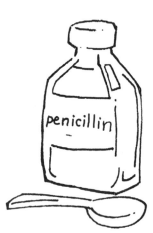

You will take it in turns to talk. Start by saying:

I am penicillin. You can't throw me overboard because ...

When everyone has finished, you can talk again. This time, try to think up arguments why another invention that has talked isn't so useful. Remember: You want someone else to be thrown overboard!

From Group Work (Intermediate) by Peter Watcyn-Jones © Penguin Books 2000

⚲ 11 The invention game

Student E

Imagine machines and other inventions or discoveries could talk. Also imagine that you are all travelling in a balloon that has a small hole in it and is falling. The only thing to do to save all the inventions is to throw one overboard. But which one?

You are a telephone. Try to think up convincing reasons why you should not be thrown overboard. For example:

Without me,

- you wouldn't be able to call the police or ambulances in an emergency
- you would find it hard to keep in touch with friends and relatives living a long way away from you

etc.

You will take it in turns to talk. Start by saying:

I am a telephone. You can't throw me overboard because ...

When everyone has finished, you can talk again. This time, try to think up arguments why another invention that has talked isn't so useful. Remember: You want someone else to be thrown overboard!

⚲ 11 The Invention Game

Student F

Imagine machines and other inventions or discoveries could talk. Also imagine that you are all travelling in a balloon that has a small hole in it and is falling. The only thing to do to save all the inventions is to throw one overboard. But which one?

You are a satellite. Try to think up convincing reasons why you should not be thrown overboard. For example:

Without me,

- you wouldn't be able to watch all the TV programmes you can now
- you wouldn't be able to use your mobile phone in many places

etc.

You will take it in turns to talk. Start by saying:

I am a satellite. You can't throw me overboard because ...

When everyone has finished, you can talk again. This time, try to think up arguments why another invention that has talked isn't so useful. Remember: You want someone else to be thrown overboard!

-2	-1	0	+1	+2
strongly disagree	**disagree**	**not sure/ can't decide**	**agree**	**strongly agree**
-2	-1	0	+1	+2
strongly disagree	**disagree**	**not sure/ can't decide**	**agree**	**strongly agree**
-2	-1	0	+1	+2
strongly disagree	**disagree**	**not sure/ can't decide**	**agree**	**strongly agree**
-2	-1	0	+1	+2
strongly disagree	**disagree**	**not sure/ can't decide**	**agree**	**strongly agree**

From *Group Work (Intermediate)* by Peter Watcyn-Jones © Penguin Books 2000

12 In my opinion ...

Men and women can never really be equal.	The future is frightening rather than exciting.
The Internet will completely change the way people work, learn, shop and do business.	Politicians are mainly interested in advancing their own careers.
It is better to take any job than to be unemployed.	English is a fairly easy language to learn.
Today's pop music is not as good as it used to be.	Smoking should be banned in all public places.
Living in a city is better than living in the country.	There are no such things as ghosts, flying saucers, etc.
There is too much money in sport nowadays.	It is better to stay single than to get married.
There are certain jobs that are not really suitable for women.	When you speak a foreign language, it doesn't matter if you make mistakes, as long as people understand you.
My country is not as nice as it was ten years ago.	You can tell a lot about a person from the clothes he/she wears.
Murderers should always be executed rather than be given life imprisonment.	Marriages work best when couples are from the same background, race and religion.
People who follow fashion are fools and probably have more money than sense.	The most important thing about a job is the money.

If you could change one thing about yourself, what would it be?	If you could travel around the world, which **five** countries would you definitely visit?
If you could be someone famous for a day, who would you be, and why?	If you could interview a famous person from history, who would you choose and why?
If you were an animal, which animal would you be and why?	If you were the head of your government, what would be the biggest problem facing you at the moment?
If you had to emigrate to another country, which would you choose and why?	If you could have one special talent, what would that be?
If money was no object, what three things would you like to own or buy?	If you were given three wishes, all of which would come true, what would you wish for?

 　　　From *Group Work (Intermediate)* by Peter Watcyn-Jones © Penguin Books 2000

13 What if ...

If you could change one thing about your life at present, what would that be?

If you could choose the plot of your dream tonight, what would that be?

If you could travel back in time and change one thing that happened in your life, what would that be?

If you had the chance to be either rich, famous, happy or very intelligent, which would you choose and why?

If you could read the private diaries of anyone the world, whose would they be and why?

If you could change one thing about your parents or someone else in your family, what would that be?

If you could have any job in the world, which would you choose and why?

If you could change one event in history, what would that be and why?

If you could uninvent something that has already been invented, what would you choose and why?

If you had to eat the same food for a whole month (and nothing else), what would you choose?

From *Group Work (Intermediate)* by Peter Watcyn-Jones © Penguin Books 2000 **Photocopiable** 41

If there was the equivalent of an Oscar for the performance (*live speeches*, etc.) of politicians, who would win the award in your country?

If you knew the world was going to end tomorrow morning, how would you spend today?

If you could be a famous film star, pop star, painter, writer, sports star or political leader, which would you choose to be and why?

If you could change one part of your body, what would that be?

If you could change one aspect of your personality, what would that be?

If it were possible to live until you were 150, when would you choose to (a) stop studying (b) get married (c) have children?

If you could wish for one of the following, which would you choose: (a) an end to war (b) an end to poverty (c) an end to natural disasters (*earthquakes, floods*, etc.)? Give reasons for your choice.

If you could choose your own first name or names, what would you choose instead of your present one(s)?

If, through plastic surgery, you could be made to look like someone else, who would you choose to look like and why?

If you could predict one event in the future, which would you choose: (a) the winning number in the next National Lottery draw (b) the date of your own death (c) the name of your future (or next) wife (d) the date and place of the next major earthquake?

14 What to look for in a job

Work in groups of three. Here are fifteen things to think about when choosing a job. Choose ten that you think are important, then rank them in order 1–10 with the most important one first. (If you cannot agree entirely, you will have to compromise.)

The most important thing about a job is:

_____ the salary

_____ the interest of the work

_____ flexi-time

_____ the people you work with

_____ the chances for promotion

_____ the work environment (clean, well-lit, etc.)

_____ the opportunity to travel

_____ the opportunity to make decisions

_____ learning new skills

_____ being close to where you live

_____ feeling you are helping other people

_____ facing new challenges

_____ its social status

_____ security

_____ the perks (company car, cheap meals, etc.)

When you have finished, compare your choices with another group. Were they very different?

Is there anything else (not mentioned above) that you think is very important when choosing a job?

From *Group Work (Intermediate)* by Peter Watcyn-Jones © Penguin Books 2000

Photocopiable   43

15 Future questionnaire ABC cards

A	B	C
A	B	C
A	B	C
A	B	C
A	B	C

From *Group Work (Intermediate)* by Peter Watcyn-Jones © Penguin Books 2000

Your friends

By 2050 your closest friend will be

A someone you met on the Internet.
B an artificial personality you made on your computer.
C a real person.

Death

By 2050 the average life expectancy will be

A less than 75.
B 75–100.
C over 100.

Computers

By 2050 computers will have changed the human race

A hardly at all.
B considerably; we'll have become much more isolated from each other.
C totally; humans will be almost a different species.

Punishment

By 2050, the death penalty will have been revived in most European countries.

A No, never.
B Yes, it's the only way to stop violent crime.
C Yes, but it will do nothing to reduce crime.

Missing talent

By 2050 which of these abilities will we rarely have any use for?

A handwriting (we'll all use keyboards).
B talking foreign languages (we'll all have translators).
C cooking (we'll all use pre-prepared meals).

Environment

By 2050 global warming will

A have disappeared – it was just a stupid scare story.
B be controlled by close international co-operation.
C have continued unchecked with terrible consequences.

Terrorism

By 2050 terrorism will have

A increased – we'll have terrorists with nuclear weapons within ten years.
B decreased – it will be defeated by international co-operation.
C stayed the same.

Crime

By 2050 the streets will be

A safer – high-tech security will have reduced crime.
B more dangerous – all criminals will have guns.
C no better – whatever the police come up with, the criminals will always be one step ahead.

Genetic engineering

By 2050 genetic engineering will

A be thought of as unnatural and we won't use it.
B enable us all to go shopping for children with any characteristic we like; it will be acceptable to have 'designer children'.
C be open only to the very, very rich and kept underground.

UFOs (flying saucers)

By 2050 the official line on UFOs will have

A changed – a major government will confess that they do exist.
B dramatically changed – a major government will admit that UFOs exist and that they knew about them all the time.
C unchanged – all governments will still deny that they exist.

⧂ 15 Future questionnaire

Cards

This present year
By 2050 we'll think the strangest thing about this present year was

A everybody worked in an office.
B everybody used cash.
C everybody drove a car.

Transport
By 2050 cars will have been

A banned from city centres.
B banned from just about everywhere you can think of.
C welcomed everywhere; they will have been reinvented as pollution-free solar cell driven buggies.

Mass destruction
If a man-made catastrophe ends the world by 2050, it's more likely to be

A a nuclear war.
B a biological war.
C everyday pollution.

Marriage
By 2050

A a computer will choose your marriage partner for you.
B only certain people will be allowed to get married.
C marriage will be replaced by a state contract, renewable annually.

Space exploration
By 2050 space exploration will

A have put men on Mars.
B have been taken over by private enterprise, and used only for making money.
C have stopped as interest runs out.

Work
By 2050

A only half the population in most countries will have a job.
B your free time will be greater than the time you spend at work.
C most people will work from home.

Appearance
By 2050 medical science will have

A cured baldness and the common cold.
B cured baldness and the common cold years before.
C still been unable to find a cure for baldness and the common cold.

The Internet
By 2050

A almost every home in the world will be linked to the Internet.
B the Internet as we know it will have been replaced by something else.
C 99% of all shopping will be done via the Internet.

Medicine/surgery
By 2050 most people will be walking around with

A no artificial parts in their bodies.
B at least one artificial part in their bodies.
C more than three artificial parts in their bodies.

Money
By 2050

A we will still have paper money and coins.
B there will be a world currency.
C 'smart' credit cards (impossible to use fraudulently and linked to your bank account) will be used for all money transactions.

Photocopiable *From Group Work (Intermediate) by Peter Watcyn-Jones © Penguin Books 2000*

Plan of zoo

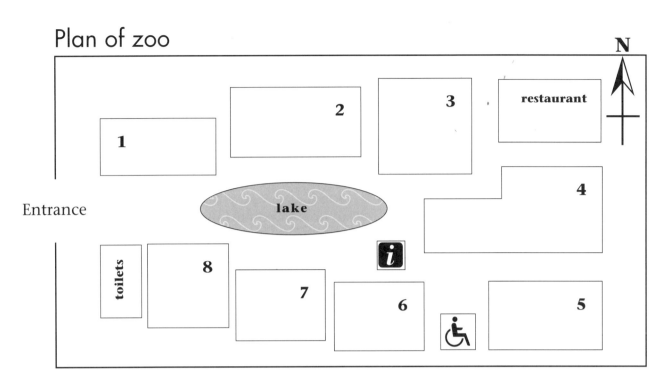

Mark in the names of the buildings and find out which one is the **Seal Enclosure**.

The Polar Bear Enclosure is near the entrance.

There are disabled toilets next to the Reptile House.

The Giraffe House is next to the Elephant House.

A

The toilets are next to the Polar Bear Enclosure.

The Information Office is **not** in front of the Gorilla House.

The Monkey House and the Gorilla House are next to each other.

B

The Seal Enclosure is south of the lake.

The Monkey House is next to the restaurant.

As you enter the zoo, the first building on your left is the Lion House.

C

The Reptile House is next to the Seal Enclosure.

If you're sitting facing south in the restaurant, you'll have a good view of the Elephant House.

The Gorilla House is north of the lake, next to the Lion House.

D

17 What's in a job? Cards

Student A

Here are 10 jobs:

a doctor, a priest, a politician, a pop star, an entertainer, a housewife, a factory worker, a teacher, a journalist, a dustman, a police officer

You have to order them 1–10 according to the salary they get. Do this on a separate piece of paper.

When you have all finished, take it in turns to read out your order. The others now try to guess on what you had based your order.

Student B

Here are 10 jobs:

a doctor, a priest, a politician, a pop star, an entertainer, a housewife, a factory worker, a teacher, a journalist, a dustman, a police officer

You have to order them 1–10 according to how important the job is to society. Do this on a separate piece of paper.

When you have all finished, take it in turns to read out your order. The others now try to guess on what you had based your order.

Student C

Here are 10 jobs:

a doctor, a priest, a politician, a pop star, an entertainer, a housewife, a factory worker, a teacher, a journalist, a dustman, a police officer

You have to order them 1–10 according to how interesting/full of variety the job is. Do this on a separate piece of paper.

When you have all finished, take it in turns to read out your order. The others now try to guess on what you had based your order.

Student D

Here are 10 jobs.

a doctor, a priest, a politician, a pop star, an entertainer, a housewife, a factory worker, a teacher, a journalist, a dustman, a police officer

You have to order them 1–10 according to how stressful the job is. Do this on a separate piece of paper.

When you have all finished, take it in turns to read out your order. The others now try to guess on what you had based your order.

Student E

Here are 10 jobs.

a doctor, a priest, a politician, a pop star, an entertainer, a housewife, a factory worker, a teacher, a journalist, a dustman, a police officer

You have to order them 1–10 according to the status of the job (in other people's eyes). Do this on a separate piece of paper.

When you have all finished, take it in turns to read out your order. The others now try to guess on what you had based your order.

Student F

Here are 10 jobs.

a doctor, a priest, a politician, a pop star, an entertainer, a housewife, a factory worker, a teacher, a journalist, a dustman, a police officer

You have to order them 1–10 according to the job you'd like to have. Do this on a separate piece of paper.

When you have all finished, take it in turns to read out your order. The others now try to guess on what you had based your order.

 From *Group Work (Intermediate)* by Peter Watcyn-Jones © Penguin Books 2000

18 Two situations

Situation 1

You have 15 minutes to think of an answer.
Imagine you could create a completely new country made up of the best things from at least five other countries. What would this country be like? What would it be called?

Think about:

- the climate (like Spain, Alaska, etc.)
- the food
- the standard of living
- the culture
- the people
- the political system
- the scenery
- the natural resources
- anything else? (specify)

Write down the details, then one of you can report to the rest of the class, e.g.

Our new country would be called ...

It will have a climate like ... (warm and sunny in the summer and ...)

It will have a standard of living like ..., etc.

 # 18 Two situations

Situation 2

You have 15 minutes to think of an answer.
Imagine you could be frozen at the time of death and brought back to life again in 200 years' time. In what ways do you think things will have changed?

Think about:

- countries
- space exploration
- life span
- transport
- computers
- family life (marriage, children, etc.)
- jobs
- homes
- anything else? (specify)

Write a paragraph to describe these changes. Then one of you can read it out to the rest of the class.

19 Pets and their owners

Find out who owns which pet.
Jack's pet came fourth.
The tortoise was fifth.
Jack's pet was a dog.

name	pet	position
		1st
		2nd
		3rd
		4th
		5th

A

Find out who owns which pet.
The cat was third.
Amanda's pet wasn't the tortoise.
Harry's parrot didn't come second.

name	pet	position
		1st
		2nd
		3rd
		4th
		5th

B

Find out who owns which pet.
Julia's pet wasn't first, but it was higher
   than the dog.
Amanda's pet didn't come second.
The tortoise was owned by Sally.

name	pet	position
		1st
		2nd
		3rd
		4th
		5th

C

Find out who owns which pet.
Harry showed a parrot and it beat the
   hamster.
Sally's pet came after the dog.
The hamster came second.

name	pet	position
		1st
		2nd
		3rd
		4th
		5th

D

 From *Group Work (Intermediate)* by Peter Watcyn-Jones © Penguin Books 2000

20 What clothes did they buy?

✂ ---

Find out who bought what and in which colour.

One man bought a black jumper.
Chris bought something green.
The shirt wasn't yellow.

name	bought	colour
Peter		
Mark		
Tom		
Bill		
Chris		

A

Find out who bought what and in which colour.

One man bought a pair of trousers.
The tie Bill bought wasn't brown.
Mark bought a shirt.

name	bought	colour
Peter		
Mark		
Tom		
Bill		
Chris		

B

Find out who bought what and in which colour.

Tom bought a pair of shoes.
Mark didn't buy the jumper or the pair
  of shoes.
One of the things bought was blue.

name	bought	colour
Peter		
Mark		
Tom		
Bill		
Chris		

C

Find out who bought what and in which colour.

The item of clothing Peter bought
  was black.
The item of clothing Mark bought
  wasn't green.
The shoes were brown.

name	bought	colour
Peter		
Mark		
Tom		
Bill		
Chris		

D

21 Situations from dialogues

Look at the following dialogue. Your task is to expand it by adding 6–8 lines both before and after the extract. You must also include a fourth character, D, somewhere. Before you start, think of the following:

1 Who are the characters? (A, B and C)
2 Where are they and why are they there?
3 What is happening now? What might have happened before and what is going to happen next?
4 Where is it best to introduce the fourth person (D) – before the extract, after the extract, or both before and after?

You can write your dialogue here:

....
....
....
....
....
....
....
....

A: **Do you mind if I join you?**

B: **No, not at all.**

A: **Thanks. (slight pause) Cigarette?**

B: **No, thanks. I don't smoke.**

A: **Do you mind if I do?**

B: **No, not at all.**

C: **But I do!**

A: **Sorry? Are you talking to me?**

C: **I certainly am. And I'd rather you didn't smoke, if you don't mind.**

B: **Oh, don't take any notice of him/her. Go ahead and smoke – there aren't any *No Smoking* signs in here.**

....
....
....
....
....
....
....
....

When you have finished, choose parts and read it out.

If you like, perform it in front of the whole class!

  From *Group Work (Intermediate)* by Peter Watcyn-Jones © Penguin Books 2000

21 Situations from dialogues

Look at the following dialogue. Your task is to expand it by adding 6–8 lines both before and after the extract. You must also include a fourth character, D, somewhere. Before you start, think of the following:

1 Who are the characters? (A, B and C)
2 Where are they and why are they there?
3 What is happening now? What might have happened before and what is going to happen next?
4 Where is it best to introduce the fourth person (D) – before the extract, after the extract, or both before and after?

You can write your dialogue here:

....

....

....

....

....

....

....

A: It's all your fault!

B: But how was I to know he'd/she'd phone?

A: You should have guessed. You know what he's/she's like.

C: Still it could be worse.

A: What do you mean?

C: Well, at least we got here, didn't we? And nobody else knows yet, do they?

A: Yes, that's right! Nobody else knows yet!

B: I suppose so. But I just wish he/she hadn't phoned.

....

....

....

....

....

....

....

....

When you have finished, choose parts and read it out.

If you like, perform it in front of the whole class!

From *Group Work (Intermediate)* by Peter Watcyn-Jones © Penguin Books 2000   **Photocopiable**

Look at the following dialogue. Your task is to expand it by adding 6–8 lines both before and after the extract. You must also include a fourth character, D, somewhere. Before you start, think of the following:

1 Who are the characters? (A, B and C)
2 Where are they and why are they there?
3 What is happening now? What might have happened before and what is going to happen next?
4 Where is it best to introduce the fourth person (D) – before the extract, after the extract, or both before and after?

You can write your dialogue here:

....
....
....
....
....
....
....
....

A: He's/She's late!
B: Maybe something's happened.
C: No, he/she would have phoned.
B: Not if he's/she's had an accident! He/She couldn't phone then!
A: Yes, you're right. What if he's/she's dead?
C: Don't talk stupid! There's probably a very good reason like the car's broken down again. You know how old his/her car is.
A: Well, we can't wait much longer.
B: Let's give him/her five minutes more. If he/she doesn't arrive, then we'll go. Agreed?
C: There's only one problem.
A: What's that?
C: He's/She's got all the documents! We can't go without those, can we?

....
....
....
....
....
....
....

When you have finished, choose parts and read it out.

If you like, perform it in front of the whole class!

 From *Group Work (Intermediate)* by Peter Watcyn-Jones © Penguin Books 2000

21 Situations from dialogues

Look at the following dialogue. Your task is to expand it by adding 6–8 lines both before and after the extract. You must also include a fourth character, D, somewhere. Before you start, think of the following:

1   Who are the characters? (A, B and C)
2   Where are they and why are they there?
3   What is happening now? What might have happened before and what is going to happen next?
4   Where is it best to introduce the fourth person (D) – before the extract, after the extract, or both before and after?

You can write your dialogue here:

....
....
....
....
....
....
....
....

A: What are you staring at?

B: Sorry? Are you talking to me?

A: Yes, you! What are you staring at?

B: What do you mean, staring? I haven't been staring at anybody?

A: Yes, you have. You've been staring at my girlfriend/boyfriend all night.

B: I'm sorry, I don't know what you're talking about.

C: I saw him/her staring too!

A: See!

B: Look, I don't know what you two are talking about. I just came in here on my own for a bit of peace and quiet, that's all! I most certainly haven't been staring at you, your boyfriend/girlfriend or anyone else.

C: You were staring at that man/woman over there too – the one by the soft drinks machine.

....
....
....
....
....
....
....
....

When you have finished, choose parts and read it out.

If you like, perform it in front of the whole class!

From *Group Work (Intermediate)* by Peter Watcyn-Jones © Penguin Books 2000   **Photocopiable**   55

22 Jigsaw reading 1

A lucky escape!

In the third year of World War I, Bavarian and French troops

faced each other in the trenches across no-man's land.

One day, Corporal Hitler of the Bavarian infantry woke

suddenly from a terrible dream. In it he had been buried

beneath an avalanche of earth and had felt blood pouring

down his chest. He found himself lying unharmed in his

trench shelter not far from the French front. All was quiet.

Nevertheless his dream worried him. He left the shelter and

moved into open country between the armies. A part of his

mind told him that he was being stupid because he could be

hit by a stray bullet. But he went forward against his will.

A sudden burst of gunfire, followed by a loud explosion, made

Corporal Hitler fall to the ground. Then he hurried back to the

shelter – but it was not there! In its place was a huge crater.

Everyone in the shelter had been buried alive. Only he

survived.

From that day on, Hitler believed that he had been entrusted

with a special mission, which promised him a great destiny

in world events.

Photocopiable From *Group Work (Intermediate)* by Peter Watcyn-Jones © Penguin Books 2000

Tina was born in 1940 in Brazil, but she has clear memories

of a previous existence as a child in France and of her own

murder by a German soldier early in World War I. She gave

an account of her death to the Brazilian Institute for Psychic

Research.

'I don't think there was anyone at home that day,' she wrote,

'because it was I who answered the door. It must have been

about ten in the morning and the weather was cloudy.' A

soldier entered, wearing a round helmet and olive-green

uniform. He carried what looked like a rifle and fired it at

her heart.

'I remember,' she continued, 'asking for water before I died,

but I don't remember if he gave me any. I can see myself lying

on the floor on my back, wearing a tight dress and lying in a

pool of blood.'

Tina has had two distinct marks from birth – on the front and

back of her left side – precisely where a bullet aimed at the

heart would have gone in and out.

A friend of mine was driving home one night along the A25

road to London when he passed a young lady standing by the

side of the road. He pulled up and asked her if she needed a

lift. Without speaking, she got into the car. He thought she

was very pretty and fancied her and tried to get her talking,

but she just wouldn't say anything, not even where she was

getting off. Instead, at the junction where she wanted him to

turn off, she pointed. Then at the road and then at her house,

where she got out of the car. He drove off, feeling rather angry

and disappointed.

A couple of days later, he was looking for something in the car

when he came across a woman's coat. Knowing it must be

the hitchhiker's, he decided to go back to the house where he

had dropped her off and return the coat. He managed to find

it and knocked at the door. A middle-aged lady opened it. He

held out the coat and explained that he wanted to return it to

the young lady – her daughter perhaps. To his surprise, the

woman burst into tears.

'Yes, it was my daughter's,' she said, 'but she was killed on

the A25 road five years ago!'

It is Monday, July 4th 1997.

An Air France Boeing 747 has just taken off and is on its way from Paris to Copenhagen.

Ten minutes into the flight, the captain reports problems with one of the engines.

Suddenly, there is an explosion and the captain realizes that the plane is going to crash.

As they near the Belgian border the plane starts losing height rapidly.

It crashes on the border between France and Belgium.

The plane splits in half. On board are 150 French passengers and 200 Belgians.

Where are the survivors buried – in France or in Belgium?

23 Jigsaw reading 2

A friend of mine was taking his motorbike driving test a few years ago.

The test involved the learner riding around various streets where, at certain points, the examiner would be watching and checking that he was doing everything correctly.

My friend was pretty nervous, but the test seemed to be going quite well.

Then the examiner stopped him and said he was about to test his emergency stop.

He told my friend to continue driving around the streets and at some point he would jump out and shout 'Stop!'

My friend set off round the streets again, and a few minutes later had completed most of the circuit, but the examiner still hadn't jumped out.

Then, when he came round the last corner, he saw a group of people in the middle of the road.

He stopped and went to see what was wrong.

They were all gathered around a body lying on the ground. It was the examiner. He was stone dead!

What do you think had happened to the examiner?

 From *Group Work (Intermediate)* by Peter Watcyn-Jones © Penguin Books 2000

A coach party from Manchester was on a day trip to the seaside town of Barmouth in North Wales.

They had a really wonderful time.

They had been on the beach, played bingo, eaten fish and chips and had finally ended up having a few drinks in the pub where they had parked their coach.

As they crossed the pub car park to get into the coach to go home they found a man who, judging by his accent, was from Manchester.

He was really drunk and could hardly stand, so they helped him onto the coach.

He fell asleep immediately and was soon snoring loudly.

When they arrived in Manchester, they woke him up and said, 'We're back in Manchester now, mate. Good thing we found you or you'd have missed the coach!'

'Manchester!' said the man. 'Oh no!'

With that, he rushed out of the coach and caught the next one back to Barmouth.

Why do you think the man wanted to return to Barmouth?

24 Letters to an advice column

Here are the answers that four people received when they wrote to the Problem Page of a magazine. Try to work out:

- who you think wrote each letter.
- what the main problem was.
- what you can guess about the people, their problems and the other people in their lives.

Letter 1

Women these days are stronger and healthier in later life than ever before. No doubt you are feeling great right now and, at 49, could probably give birth to a baby with ease. The point is, though, could you manage a 10-year-old at 59 or a 14-year-old at 63? Try to project yourself into the future and think really hard before you decide to have another baby. And I'm not surprised your husband isn't too keen - he is after all old enough to be a grandfather.

Letter 2

I'm sorry to say this but it seems to me as if you deserve to be in such a state. Not once have you admitted any responsibility for the breakdown of your marriage. Maybe you need to learn how to survive on your own before you are fit to live with anyone else. I suggest you look at your current crisis as a chance to put things right. It may not be too late to save your marriage, but you're going to have to be willing to change a lot. For a start, ask yourself not what your wife can do for you, but what you can do for your wife. Take this opportunity to learn some practical skills such as cooking, ironing, and so on. And if you decide that it's your wife you want back and not just a housekeeper, then set out to woo her back.

Letter 3

This is a common problem, so don't allow the school to ignore it. Getting everyone involved - the teachers, your daughter, the other girl and her parents - to work out why it's happening is often the best way to deal with it. People often throw their weight about at school because they're having a hard time at home. And your daughter may be sending out signals to this girl that she'll lie down and take all the bullying. Try to see how and why your daughter and this girl are locked into this game and you might be able to help both of them stop it happening. But don't keep quiet and ignore it as your husband suggests because bullying thrives on silence.

Letter 4

Don't always trust people who phone up anonymously - they may just want to cause trouble for some reason. Give your boyfriend a chance by asking him to sit down with you to talk it over. After all, he did admit to a previous affair. But you really only have three options: sort it out and rebuild your trust in him; go on as you are and suffer in silence; or kick him out. If he avoids talking to you and he continues to work late, then I know which one I'd choose.

Photocopiable *From Group Work (Intermediate)* by Peter Watcyn-Jones © Penguin Books 2000

25 An interview

Work in groups of three. Here are fifteen answers given in an interview. Think of questions that fit these answers and then decide what the person who was interviewed was like.

1 _____ ?

Yes, about two and a half years ago.

2 _____ ?

Yes, that's correct.

3 _____ ?

No, not exactly. Only eleven years younger.

4 _____ ?

Not at all.

5 _____ ?

I'd rather not answer that question, if you don't mind.

6 _____ ?

Five times. But I know it'll be different this time.

7 _____ ?

Somewhere exotic. Thailand or Bali or maybe the Caribbean.

8 _____ ?

Perhaps. I really haven't made my mind up yet.

9 _____ ?

I think that's my business, don't you?

10 _____ ?

I'm sorry. I haven't the foggiest idea what you're talking about.

11 _____ ?

That's a damn lie!

12 _____ ?

Well, I was very young then.

13 _____ ?

Not a bit. I'd do the same thing again if I had to.

14 _____ ?

No, of course not!

15 _____ ?

You print that and I'll sue you for libel!!

When you have finished, compare your answers with another group.

From *Group Work (Intermediate)* by Peter Watcyn-Jones © Penguin Books 2000

Q 26 UK quiz

Team name: _____

Score

1 **What is the population of the United Kingdom?**

   (a) less than 50 million (b) between 50–60 million (c) over 60 million

2 **Who normally lives at the following places?**

   (a) Buckingham Palace   _____

   (b) 10 Downing Street   _____

3 **London is the capital of England. What are the capitals of:**

   (a) Scotland   _____

   (b) Wales   _____

   (c) Northern Ireland   _____

4 **Match up the following places with what they are famous for.**

Place	Famous for
1 Baker Street	a tennis
2 St. Andrew's	b famous football ground
3 Ascot	c where Sherlock Holmes lived
4 Wimbledon	d old university town
5 Loch Ness	e horse racing
6 Llangollen	f a sea monster
7 Wembley Stadium	g golf
8 Cambridge	h an international music festival

5 **Name the two main political parties in the UK.**

   (a) _____   (b) _____

6 **London is the largest city in the UK. Which of the following is the second largest?**

   (a) Manchester **(b)** Liverpool **(c)** Birmingham **(d)** Brighton

7 **In which town in England was William Shakespeare born?**

   (a) London **(b)** Stratford-upon-Avon **(c)** Oxford

8 **At what age in Britain can you legally do the following things?**

   (a) learn to drive   _____

   (b) vote   _____

   (c) leave school   _____

   (d) buy/drink alcohol   _____

   (e) get married (with parent's permission)   _____

 From *Group Work (Intermediate)* by Peter Watcyn-Jones © Penguin Books 2000

 **26 UK quiz**

Score

9 Do British policemen normally carry guns?   Yes ☐   No ☐ ||||⟶ ☐

10 Match up the following colloquial words with more usual ones. ||||⟶ ☐

Colloquial word	**Usual word**
1 a quid	a an umbrella
2 a fag	b a television set
3 a cuppa	c a (short) sleep
4 a loo	d £1
5 a telly	e a toilet
6 plonk	f a cigarette
7 a kip	g a cup of tea
8 a brolly	h cheap wine

11 Name two British daily newspapers. ||||⟶ ☐

(a) _____   (b) _____

12 Look at the map. Mark the places A–J. Choose from the following (not all are used):

Rivers	**Countries**	**Islands**	**Towns**	
River Avon	England	Anglesey	Belfast	Glasgow
River Severn	Scotland	Isle of Man	Birmingham	Liverpool
River Thames	Wales	Isle of Wight	Brighton	London
Mountains	N. Ireland	Jersey	Cambridge	Oxford
Ben Nevis			Cardiff	York
Snowdon				

Answers:

A _____

B _____

C _____

D _____

E _____

F _____

G _____

H _____

I _____

J _____ ||||⟶ ☐

Final score ☐

Q 27 An alternative quiz

Team sheets

Team: _____

Team: _____

Q1 _____	Q1 _____
Q2 _____	Q2 _____
Q3 _____	Q3 _____
Q4 _____	Q4 _____
Q5 _____	Q5 _____
Q6 _____	Q6 _____
Q7 _____	Q7 _____
Q8 _____	Q8 _____
Q9 _____	Q9 _____
Q10 _____	Q10 _____
Q11 _____	Q11 _____
Q12 _____	Q12 _____
Q13 _____	Q13 _____
Q14 _____	Q14 _____
Q15 _____	Q15 _____
Q16 _____	Q16 _____
Q17 _____	Q17 _____
Q18 _____	Q18 _____
Q19 _____	Q19 _____
Q20 _____	Q20 _____

Final score: [ ]

Final score: [ ]

From *Group Work (Intermediate)* by Peter Watcyn-Jones © Penguin Books 2000

Read out the following, allowing time for the groups to write down their answers. Do not read out the answers yet!

1 Name a game played either on the beach or at a picnic. (**volleyball**)

2 Name a job that involves climbing ladders. (**window cleaner**)

3 Name a topic of conversation on a first date. (**jobs**)

4 Name something you eat at the cinema. (**popcorn**)

5 Name something you have more than one of in the bathroom. (**toothbrush**)

6 Name something you associate with Spain. (**bull fighting**)

7 Name any subject which families argue over? (**money**)

8 Name something which has a handle on it. (**door**)

9 Name a glamorous job. (**model**)

10 Name something which requires a signature. (**cheque**)

11 Name something white. (**snow**)

12 Name something people can have improved by plastic surgery. (**nose**)

13 Name a food associated with Italy. (**spaghetti**)

14 Name something which comes in pairs. (**shoes**)

15 Name a type of musical instrument which you blow. (**trumpet**)

16 Name something a stranger on the street might ask you for. (**the time**)

17 Name something that works with a battery. (**torch**)

18 Name an item you would take on holiday with you. (**swimsuit**)

19 Name something that people are frightened of. (**the dark**)

20 Name something you would do if you won the Lottery. (**travel/go on holiday**)

Tell the students to change papers with another group. Now read out the 'correct' answers. They get 1 point for each correct answer.

Follow up questions

Who scored the most?

Were there any answers that surprised you?

The 100 people questioned were British. Would the answers have been different, do you think, if the people who answered were from your country?

Read out the following, allowing time for the groups to write down their answers. Do not read out the answers yet!

1. Name a household chore done at least once a week. (**washing clothes**)

2. Apart from a waltz, name any other type of dance. (**Tango**)

3. Name a dangerous instrument for a naked musician. (**cymbals**)

4. Name an irritating or annoying habit. (**nail biting/biting nails**)

5. Name an excuse for leaving a party when you're not enjoying it. (**feeling unwell/feeling ill**)

6. Name somewhere where you would you see a 'No Smoking' sign. (**on a train**)

7. Name the most attractive feature in a man. (**his eyes**)

8. Name one of the colours of the rainbow. (**red**)

9. Name something often smuggled through Customs. (**drugs**)

10. Name something a man likes to show off. (**his car**)

11. Name a famous painter/artist living or dead. (**Van Gogh**)

12. Name something you like doing which is not good for you. (**eating sweets/chocolates**)

13. Name your favourite day of the week. (**Saturday**)

14. Name a job you'd hate to have. (**undertaker**)

15. Name the first thing you do when you wake up in the morning. (**stretch**)

16. Name something that is considered bad luck. (**walking under a ladder**)

17. Name a state in America. (**Texas**)

18. Name something that would embarrass you. (**falling over**)

19. Name a play by Shakespeare. (**Hamlet**)

20. Name a musical instrument you could easily play in the bath. (**mouth organ/harmonica**)

Tell the students to change papers with another group. Now read out the 'correct' answers. They get 1 point for each correct answer.

Follow up questions

Who scored the most?

Were there any answers that surprised you?

The 100 people questioned were British. Would the answers have been different, do you think, if the people who answered were from your country?

    From *Group Work (Intermediate)* by Peter Watcyn-Jones © Penguin Books 2000

Q 28 True or false?

Betting slips;
True/False cards

50

100

40

90

30

80

20

70

10

60

FALSE

TRUE

From *Group Work (Intermediate)* by Peter Watcyn-Jones © Penguin Books 2000

Photocopiable

69

1 We walk our dogs but in China they walk with birds in their cages, and hang them in trees to let the birds enjoy the fresh air and scenery.
True. Groups of mostly old men with bird cages gather in the parks at dawn.

2 Three villages in France and one in Spain have changed their names to Champagne to enable their sparkling wine to be sold under that name.
False.

3 An ant removed from its ant hill and released several kilometres from home will find its way back by its sense of smell.
True.

4 Crying was quite a manly thing during the Middle Ages. A crying man was considered tough and impressive.
True. A man who wouldn't cry in public was considered to be quite strange.

5 Michael Jackson sent a costume for his wax model at Madame Tussaud's and the staff, who were unaware that he only wears one sequined glove, spent £1,000 making a matching one.
False.

6 In 1956, the crew of a Japanese whaling boat discovered a living person in the stomach of a whale they had just caught.
False

7 A camel's hump contains sufficient water for the animal to walk a distance of 2,000 kilometres, without taking a drink.
False. A camel's hump does not contain water. It is full of fat.

8 In the film *Singing in the Rain*, Gene Kelly danced his way through a shower of diluted milk because it showed up better on film than pure water.
True.

9 If they want to keep their jobs, Malaysian Airlines stewardesses must not put on any weight after being hired.
False.

10 Ivan the Terrible had the eyes of the architects of St Basil's Cathedral poked out to stop them from ever creating a more beautiful building.
True. Ivan loved the cathedral and wanted it to be the most beautiful building in the world.

11 In China it is illegal to dance cheek to cheek in public.
False. It was considered indecent at one time, but owing to increasing western influence it is becoming accepted.

12 Ian Fleming, the author of the James Bond books, began writing to cure his alcoholism. His doctor told him to take up writing so that he would have something else to think about.
True.

13 On a Philippine island, almost 30 years after World War II ended, a Japanese soldier was found who refused to surrender because he thought that the war was still going on.
True. Hiroo Onada was found in 1974.

14 Before getting into politics, Fidel Castro worked as an extra in cheap Hollywood comedies.
True.

15 Once when Ronald Reagan was speaking from a balcony at the White House, his false teeth fell out and dropped into the crowd below. He never got them back.
False.

16 There are over 100 species of snake in New Zealand, and nearly 90% are poisonous.
False. There are no snakes in New Zealand.

17 Early motorists in England had to have a man walking in front of them carrying a red flag during the day and a red lamp at night.
True. The speed limit was consequently set at 4 mph.

18 In 1890, the Emperor of Abyssinia read about the introduction of the electric chair in the USA and ordered three. He then tested them by executing his chef and two of his generals.
False. He was unable to use the chairs because Abyssinia had no electricity.

19 The lack of Buddhist clergymen in Japan has prompted a cemetery in Yokohama to acquire a robot priest to conduct funerals.
True. Its eyes blink and its mouth moves, as it sings Buddhist Sutras and is programmed for ten different services.

20 The sari, a traditional Indian garment worn by women, was originally a cloth they used to wrap around dead people.
False.

21 It was fashionable in the 19th century to wear dentures (false teeth) made from the teeth of men who had died in battle.
True. Even though artificial dentures were available, 'Waterloo teeth' as they were called after the Battle of Waterloo, were preferred by fashionable gentlemen.

22 In Daniel Defoe's famous book *Robinson Crusoe*, Crusoe takes off all his clothes to swim out to the ship, but still has pockets to put things in when he gets there.
True.

23 In Thailand, many elderly people find new partners at special discos for senior citizens. Recently, a 105-year-old man met his new wife at one. She was only 92.
False.

24 Food left behind in the Antarctic by a Swedish expedition in 1901 was still fresh enough to be eaten by a British expedition 45 years later.
True. The extreme cold and the sterile atmosphere had prevented decay.

25 Like Hollywood, São Paulo in Brazil has a street where famous people have their handprints immortalised in the pavement. But this time it's soccer players, such as Pélé, and so on.
False.

26 Worldwide, people drink more Coca-Cola than any other drink.
False. Most people drink water.

27 Smokers snore more often than non-smokers because their blood contains less oxygen.
True.

28 Almost all North American Indians have the same blood group.
True. They have type O.

29 Counting up to a billion will take a person 75 years, that is, a lifetime.
False. It will take approximately 160,000 years.

30 In 1941, when Thomas Edison, inventor of the lightbulb was buried, all the lights in the USA were turned off.
True. It was President Hoover's idea.

31 The inscription on Ernest Hemingway's tomb reads: 'Excuse me for not standing up.'
False. It was his wish, but it was not done.

32 At cinemas in Colombia, roasted ants are as common a snack as popcorn.
True.

33 In 1934, Mickey Mouse received more fan mail than any other Hollywood star.
True.

34 Charlie Chaplin often kept his false teeth in whisky overnight to improve their taste.
False.

35 The famous painter, Salvador Dali, was once so poor that he used hair from his own moustache to make paint brushes.
False.

36 Fingers Wilson was a burglar in London in the late sixties. He had trained a snake to slither into buildings through cracks and then to open window catches and let him in.
False.

37 You can tell the age of a ladybird by counting the number of spots on its back.
False.

38 In Bucharest, pedestrian crossing lights have been installed which, when they are green, play the music from old Laurel and Hardy films.
True. The music tells blind people when it is safe to cross the street.

39 The supermarket shopping trolley is the second most numerous four-wheeled vehicle in the world after the car.
True.

40 Snow has only fallen once in the history of Singapore – on February 18th, 1936.
False. Singapore is on the Equator and has never seen snow.

Q 28 True or false?

Score card

Group **A**

Question	Bet	New total
		1000 *points*
1	_____	_____
2	_____	_____
3	_____	_____
4	_____	_____
5	_____	_____
6	_____	_____
7	_____	_____
8	_____	_____
9	_____	_____
10	_____	_____

Final score: _____
points

Group **B**

Question	Bet	New total
		1000 *points*
1	_____	_____
2	_____	_____
3	_____	_____
4	_____	_____
5	_____	_____
6	_____	_____
7	_____	_____
8	_____	_____
9	_____	_____
10	_____	_____

Final score: _____
points

Photocopiable

From *Group Work (Intermediate)* by Peter Watcyn-Jones © Penguin Books 2000

Q 29 Vocabulary quiz

Answer sheet

Team name: _____

		Score

1 food ☐
alcohol ☐
money ☐ ⟹ ☐

2 a clumsy person ☐
a keen gardener ☐
a DIY (do-it-yourself) expert ☐ ⟹ ☐

3 o_____ ⟹ ☐

4 (a) _____
(b) _____
(c) _____
(d) _____ ⟹ ☐

5 Your answer
_____ ⟹ ☐

(a) **(b)**

(c) **(d)**

Score

6 (a) d_____
(b) p_____
(c) a_____ ⟹ ☐

7 pie ☐ cake ☐ cheese ☐ ⟹ ☐

8 (a) o_____
(b) a_____
(c) v_____ ⟹ ☐

9 (a) _____
(b) _____
(c) _____ ⟹ ☐

10 (a) libel ☐ (b) slander ☐ ⟹ ☐

11 (a) even if it was raining. ☐
(b) even though it was raining. ☐
(c) because it was raining. ☐ ⟹ ☐

12

bleat	nag
☐	☐
bray	**purr**
☐	☐
snigger	**low**
☐	☐
snorkel	**neigh**
☐	☐

⟹ ☐

Final score
(maximum 25 points) ☐

From *Group Work (Intermediate)* by Peter Watcyn-Jones © Penguin Books 2000

Question 1

Which would a miser be interested in?
Would it be food, alcohol or money?
Mark one of the boxes.

Answer

money (1 point) A miser is a person who
likes to hoard and never spend money.

Question 2

Look at the descriptions of three types of
people in question 2. Which of these could
be described as being 'all fingers and
thumbs'?

Answer

a clumsy person (1 point)

Question 3

My sister is very stubborn. Which word
beginning with the letter 'o' is a synonym
for stubborn?

Answer

obstinate (1 point)

Question 4

I'm now going to test your spelling. Four
words altogether. Write your answers next
to a, b, c and d.

Here's the first word:
  The incident caused a lot of
  embarrassment. Spell **embarrassment**.
  Write your answer next to (a).
Here is the second word:
  She isn't a friend – she's just an
  acquaintance. Spell **acquaintance**.
  Write your answer next to (b).
Here is the third word:
  What sort of accommodation is
  available? Spell **accommodation**. Write
  your answer next to (c).
And here is the last word:
  He went to Japan on business. Spell
  business. Write your answer next to (d).

(1 point for each correct answer.
Total 4 points.)

Question 5

Look at the four drawings of insects.
Which one is a ladybird? Is it a, b, c or d?
Mark your answer.

Answer

(a) (1 point)

Question 6

I'm going to read out three things. Mark
next to a, b and c the person who would
normally use them.

Here is the first one:
  A stethoscope. Who would normally use
  a stethoscope? Write your answer next to
  (a). It begins with the letter 'd'.
Here is the second one:
  A truncheon. Who would normally use a
  truncheon? Write your answer next to
  (b). It begins with the letter 'p'.
And here is the last one:
  An easel. Who would normally use an
  easel? Write your answer next to (c). It
  begins with the letter 'a'.

Answers

(a) A stethoscope is used by a doctor or a
    nurse. It is used to listen to a patient's
    chest, heart, etc.
(b) A truncheon is used by British police
    officers (policemen/policewomen).
    They use it to protect themselves.
(c) An easel is used by an artist. It's the
    wooden frame a painting rests on.

(1 point for each correct answer.
Total 3 points)

Question 7

I'm going to read you a sentence now. How
would you finish it? Choose one of the
answers (a, b or c). Here's the sentence: The
exam was really easy. It was a piece of what?
a piece of pie, a piece of cake, or a piece of
cheese? It means the exam was very easy!

Answer

(b) cake (1 point)

        From *Group Work (Intermediate)* by Peter Watcyn-Jones © Penguin Books 2000

Question 8

I'm now going to give you definitions for three words.

Here's the first word:
  Which verb beginning with the letter 'o' means to drive past another vehicle? Write your answer next to (a).
Here is the second word:
  Which adjective beginning with the letter 'a' means happening once a year? Write your answer next to (b).
And here is the last word:
  Which noun beginning with the letter 'v' means someone who has been attacked, robbed or murdered ? Write your answer next to (c).

Answers
(a) overtake
(b) annual
(c) victim

(1 point for each correct answer. Total 3 points.)

Question 9

Name three vegetables that begin with the letter 'c'. Write your answers next to a, b and c.

Answers
Suggestions: cabbage, cauliflower, carrot, courgette, cucumber, celery, chives, chicory

(1 point for each correct answer. Total 3 points.)

Question 10

Which of the two words, (a) or (b), would be correct in this sentence:
  If you print that about me I'll sue you for libel.
  OR
  If you print that about me I'll sue you for slander.

Answer
(a) libel (1 point)

libel = writing or printing untrue statements about a person, usually to damage their reputation.

slander = saying untrue things about a person, again in order to damage their reputation.

Question 11

I'm going to read you the opening words of a sentence. You have to decide what the closing words are. There are three possible endings, but only one of them is correct. Here is the beginning of the sentence:
  She refused to take an umbrella …
Choose the correct ending.

Answer
(b) even though it was raining (1 point.)

Question 12

Look at the eight words in the boxes. Choose five that are sounds made by animals.

Answer
The five verbs are: bleat, bray, low, neigh and purr

(1 point for each verb. 5 points total.)

Extra information
bleat = sound made by a sheep or a lamb

bray = sound made by a donkey

low = sound made by a cow

neigh = sound made by a horse

purr = sound made by a cat when it is happy or contented

The other verbs mean the following:
nag = keep complaining to someone about their behaviour or asking them to do something in a way that is annoying

snigger = laugh quietly, often unkindly, at something which is not supposed to be funny

snorkel = to swim under water using a snorkel, i.e. a tube that allows a swimmer to breathe air underwater

The maximum score for this quiz is 25 points.

30 Explain the words

A

40 points
a **skinny** secretary

30 points
a black **beret**

20 points
lukewarm water

50 points
a **pushy** mother

B

60 points
a **gifted** musician

40 points
a **former** President

50 points
a **hostile** reception

50 points
a terrible **hangover**

40 points
a **monotonous** job

20 points
to **detest** housework

40 points
a £10,000 **ransom**

10 points
a **rude** child

40 points
an **uninhabited** island

20 points
to **put off** a meeting

20 points
a **huge** garden

10 points
to **hijack** a plane

30 points
a **witty** teacher

10 points
to **cure** a disease

40 points
a **superstitious** neighbour

40 points
an active **volcano**

20 points
a **delicious** meal

60 points
to **call off** a pop concert

50 points
a **shallow** river

40 points
a bad **conscience**

30 points
to **sack** a worker

40 points
a **fragrant** perfume

60 points
a terrible **drought**

10 points
a **spoilt** child

20 points
a **depressing** film

60 points
a £10 million **profit**

50 points
to **overhear** a conversation

30 points
an old **acquaintance**

D

C

From *Group Work (Intermediate)* by Peter Watcyn-Jones © Penguin Books 2000

Cards

football	by car	lonely	this morning
Hong Kong	Portugal	pink	last night
Bill Clinton	a spider	bananas	Mozart
a mouse	carrots	John Lennon	in December
I hate you!	Sorry!	hungry	What's the time?
beer	in 1996	next year	my mother
No, thanks.	No, I can't.	Yes, always.	a computer
three days ago	Happy New Year!	Good luck!	the station
Hamlet	worried	in love	Jupiter
go skiing	Keep the change!	chimney	in hospital

mouse	birthday	film	umbrella
cake	sports car	dog	hide
theatre	jeans	doctor	brother
fat	hungry	wedding	village
football	apples	garden	kiss
happy	seaside	hospital	flat
jealous	ill	motorway	thief
keep fit	museum	cash a cheque	river
mosquito	cigarette	nervous	young
Amsterdam	party	smile	police officer
quarrel	supermarket	earthquake	scared
Chinese take-away	chase	university	snake
hit	Help!	pilot	refuse

Photocopiable   *From Group Work (Intermediate)* by Peter Watcyn-Jones © Penguin Books 2000

33 Three-in-a-row: What's the question?

1	2	3	4	5
◯	◯	◯	◯	◯
6	**7**	**8**	**9**	**10**
◯	◯	◯	◯	◯
11	**12**	**13**	**14**	**15**
◯	◯	◯	◯	◯
16	**17**	**18**	**19**	**20**
◯	◯	◯	◯	◯
21	**22**	**23**	**24**	**25**
◯	◯	◯	◯	◯

33 Three-in-a-row: What's the question?

A: Spanish.

Q: What language is spoken in Spain?/What language do they speak in Spain?

A: It is a type of dog.

Q: What is a Poodle?

A: 365 or sometimes 366.

Q: How many days are there in a year?

A: He was a famous film director.

Q: Who was Alfred Hitchcock?

A: It's the capital of Belgium.

Q: What is Brussels?

A: It has six legs.

Q: How many legs does a spider have?/How many legs has a spider got?

A: It's yellow.

Q: What colour is a daffodil?

A: He was a German composer who went deaf.

Q: Who was Beethoven?

A: Mount Everest.

Q: What is the highest mountain in the world?/What is the world's highest mountain (called)?

A: It's green.

Q: What colour is grass?

A: It's a fruit?

Q: What is a pear?

A: It's short for Michael.

Q: What is Mike (Mick) short for?

A: 28, sometimes 29.

Q: How many days are there in February?

A: He was one of the Beatles.

Q: Who was John Lennon?

A: It's a type of vegetable.

Q: What is a carrot?

A: It's one of the countries of South-East Asia.

Q: What is Vietnam?

A: It has four strings.

Q: How many strings does a violin have?/How many strings are there on a violin?

A: It's in New York.

Q: Where is the Empire State Building?

A: He was a Dutch painter who cut his ear off.

Q: Who was Van Gough?

A: It's a woodwind instrument.

Q: What is a flute?

 From *Group Work (Intermediate)* by Peter Watcyn-Jones © Penguin Books 2000

33 Three-in-a-row: What's the question?

A: It's a popular pet in Britain. **Q:** What is a hamster?	**A:** It's a synonym for 'awful'. **Q:** What is 'terrible'?	**A:** There are eighteen. **Q:** How many holes are there on a golf course?	**A:** It's in California. **Q:** Where is Los Angeles?
A: It's someone who hates spending money. **Q:** What is a miser?	**A:** It's the opposite of 'sharp'. **Q:** What is 'blunt'?	**A:** He was assassinated in Dallas. **Q:** How was John F Kennedy (President Kennedy) killed?/ How did John F Kennedy (President Kennedy) die?	**A:** Bless you! **Q:** What do (should/can) you say if someone sneezes?
A: It's a type of car. **Q:** What is a Rolls-Royce?	**A:** Every four years. **Q:** How often are the Olympic Games (held)?	**A:** It's a type of bird. **Q:** What is a pigeon?	**A:** A hundred. **Q:** How many years are there in a century?
A: There are eleven on the pitch. **Q:** How many players are there in a football (soccer) team?	**A:** It's something usually worn by a man. **Q:** What is a tie?	**A:** It's next to Germany. **Q:** Where is Poland?	**A:** Shakespeare. **Q:** Who wrote *Romeo and Juliet?*
A: The British Prime Minister lives there. **Q:** Who lives at 10 Downing Street?	**A:** It's a famous Scottish drink. **Q:** What is whisky?	**A:** It's famous for films. **Q:** What is Hollywood famous for?	**A:** Bacon and eggs, usually. **Q:** What do you (usually) have for breakfast?

33 Three-in-a-row: What's the question?

A: £62.50 a night, including breakfast. **Q:** How much is the room?	**A:** Seven. **Q:** How many days are there in a week?	**A:** It's called Boxing Day. **Q:** What is December 26th called?	**A:** Cathy@netto.com **Q:** What is your (her) e-mail address?
A: A beer, please. **Q:** What would you like (do you want) to drink?	**A:** The Nile. **Q:** What is the longest river in the world?/ What is the world's longest river?	**A:** Tennis. **Q:** What do they play at Wimbledon?	**A:** No, just sugar, please. **Q:** Do you take milk and sugar?
A: Dublin. **Q:** What is the capital of Ireland?	**A:** It's white. **Q:** What colour is snow?	**A:** 0170–534321. **Q:** What is your phone number?	**A:** Jones. **Q:** What is your (his/her) surname?

Photocopiable   *From Group Work (Intermediate) by Peter Watcyn-Jones © Penguin Books 2000*

Name **five** adjectives to describe people (e.g. *friendly*).	Name **five** things you can do to keep fit.	Name **five** buildings found in a town.
Name **five** creatures with four legs.	Name **five** crimes.	Name **five** diseases or illnesses.
Name **five** garden tools.	Name **five** herbs or spices.	Name **five** hobbies.
Name **five** insects.	Name **five** items of jewellery.	Name **five** jobs or occupations.
Name **five** kinds of fruit.	Name **five** kinds of tools.	Name **five** makes of cars.
Name **five** kinds of vegetables.	Name **five** languages.	Name **five** musical instruments.

34 The category game

Cards 2

Name **five** parts of a car.	Name **five** parts of the body.	Name **five** people who wear a uniform.
Name **five** sports and games.	Name **five** things found in a school.	Name **five** things found in the kitchen.
Name **five** things people keep in a fridge.	Name **five** things made of wood.	Name **five** things that are hard.
Name **five** things that are red.	Name **five** things that can fit in your pocket.	Name **five** things that didn't exist 50 years ago.
Name **five** things that have keys.	Name **five** things that live in the sea.	Name **five** things that use electricity.
Name **five** things that are bad for you.	Name **five** things worn by men.	Name **five** things worn by women.

  From *Group Work (Intermediate)* by Peter Watcyn-Jones © Penguin Books 2000

Name **five** things you can drink.	Name **five** things you can eat.	Name **five** types of transport.
Name **five** verbs to do with moving (e.g. *walk*).	Name **five** wild animals.	Name **five** types of dances.
Name **five** things you associate with Japan.	Name **five** things that are heavy.	Name **five** verbs to do with speaking (e.g. *talk*)
Name **five** things a woman has in her handbag.	Name **five** adjectives to describe moods and feelings (e.g. *depressed*)	Name **five** words to do with money.
Name **five** things found in the bathroom.	Name **five** jobs that are well-paid.	Name **five** items of furniture.
Name **five** tourist attractions in your country.	Name **five** things that are round.	Name **five** things people are often afraid of.

34 The category game

Answer sheet

Round 1

1 _____
2 _____
3 _____
4 _____
5 _____

Score: _____

Round 2

1 _____
2 _____
3 _____
4 _____
5 _____

Score: _____

Round 3

1 _____
2 _____
3 _____
4 _____
5 _____

Score: _____

Round 4

1 _____
2 _____
3 _____
4 _____
5 _____

Score: _____

Round 5

1 _____
2 _____
3 _____
4 _____
5 _____

Score: _____

Round 6

1 _____
2 _____
3 _____
4 _____
5 _____

Score: _____

Round 7

1 _____
2 _____
3 _____
4 _____
5 _____

Score: _____

Round 8

1 _____
2 _____
3 _____
4 _____
5 _____

Score: _____

Round 9

1 _____
2 _____
3 _____
4 _____
5 _____

Score: _____

Round 10

1 _____
2 _____
3 _____
4 _____
5 _____

Score: _____

   From *Group Work (Intermediate)* by Peter Watcyn-Jones © Penguin Books 2000

The crossword below is only half filled in. Group B also has a crossword that is only half filled in. Take it in turns to ask what the missing words are, e.g. *What's 3 Down?* and answer by trying to explain each word.

```
    [1]A  F  R [2]A  I  D           [3]
          [1]A  F  R  A  I  D
                   S           [4]
       [5]   [6]C  T
             C  U  T  O
             U  T  O       [7]B  O  R  E [8]D
 [9]S  O  B  E  R  N                   E
             R  I                      
             I  O  N                   
[10]         O  S  I                   
             U  S                      
             U  S [11]H           [12]
[13]T        S  E  D              [14]
 E           S  E  D           [15]G
 N        [16]U             [17]P  E  C  K  I  S  H
[18]S  L  E  E  P  Y               D
 E           U  S                  D
          [19]    E                Y
             S  E                  
             E  T                  
             T                     
```

Before you start, make sure you know what the following words mean.
(They are all adjectives to describe moods, states and feelings.)

afraid	peckish
astonished	sleepy
bored	sober
curious	tense
giddy	upset

The crossword below is only half filled in. Group A also has a crossword that is only half filled in. Take it in turns to ask what the missing words are, e.g. *What's 2 Down?* and answer by trying to explain each word.

Before you start, make sure you know what the following words mean. (They are all adjectives to describe moods, states and feelings.)

angry	homesick
ashamed	lonely
embarrassed	nervous
excited	relieved
drunk	shocked

     From Group Work (Intermediate) by Peter Watcyn-Jones © Penguin Books 2000

36 Complete the drawing

Group sheet

36 Complete the drawing

Group sheet

  From *Group Work (Intermediate)* by Peter Watcyn-Jones © Penguin Books 2000

? 37 The trivia game

Try to guess which words are missing from the sentences below.

1 The vocabulary of the average person consists of between _____ and _____ words.

2 A study at the University of Iowa has discovered that looking at naked people can stop you from _____.

3 About _____ per cent of the world's population is left-handed.

4 Offered a new pen to write with, 97 per cent of people will write _____.

5 The average person falls asleep in _____ minutes.

6 The most common first name in the world is _____.

7 The world's oldest flag is the flag of _____, which has remained unchanged since about the year 1219.

8 Saudi Arabia covers an area of 830,000 square miles, yet there is not a single _____ in the whole country.

9 Throughout the civilized world there has only been _____ years of peace since 1496 B.C.

10 Unlike many other animals, elephants cannot _____.

11 A polar bear can smell you _____ miles away.

12 The Emperor Napoleon was terrified of _____.

13 George Washington was the first person to wear false teeth. He used to soak them in _____ at night to improve their flavour.

14 King Louis XIV of France was the first person, male or female, to wear _____.

15 In Turkey in the 16th and 17th centuries, anyone caught drinking _____ was put to death.

16 The most frequently used word in the English language is _____. The word most often used in English conversation, however, is _____.

17 In Tibet, the traditional greeting is a low bow followed by _____ three times.

18 More books are sold per head of the population in _____ than anywhere else in the world.

19 A poll of 3,000 Americans found that for 41 per cent, the thing they're most afraid of is _____. While 32 per cent stated they were afraid of heights.

20 The artist Vincent van Gogh didn't start drawing until he was _____ years old.

? 38 Choral reading

ALL: **GREEDYGUTS** by Kit Wright

SOLO 1:   I sat in the café and sipped at a Coke

There sat down beside me a WHOPPING great bloke

Who sighed as he elbowed me into the wall:

SOLO 2:   'Your trouble, my boy*, is your belly's too small!   **(Use girl if Solo 1 is female.)*

Your bottom's too thin! Take a lesson from me:

I may not be nice, but I'm GREAT, you'll agree,

And I've lasted a lifetime by playing this hunch:

ALL: *The bigger the breakfast, the larger the lunch!*

SOLO 2:   The larger the lunch, then the bigger the supper.

The deeper the teapot, the vaster the cuppa.

The fatter the sausage, the fuller the tea.

The MORE on the table, the BETTER for ME!'

ALL: His elbows moved in and his elbows moved out,

His belly grew bigger, chins wobbled about,

As forkful by forkful and plate after plate

He ate and he ate and he ate and he ATE!

SOLO 1:   I hardly could breathe, I was squashed out of shape,

So under the table I made my escape.

SOLO 2:   'Aha!'

ALL: he rejoiced,

SOLO 2:   'when it's put to the test,

The fellow who's fattest will come off the best!

Remember, my boy*, when it comes to the crunch: **(See above note.)*

ALL: *The bigger the breakfast, the larger the lunch!*

SOLO 2:   The larger the lunch, then the bigger the supper.

The deeper the teapot, the vaster the cuppa.

The fatter the sausage, the fuller the tea.

The MORE on the table, the BETTER for ME!

ALL: A lady came by who was scrubbing the floor

With a mop and a bucket.

SOLO 1:   To even the score,

I lifted that bucket of water and said,

As I poured the whole lot of it over his head:

'*I've* found all my life, it's a pretty sure bet:

ALL: The FULLER the bucket, the WETTER you GET!'

(From *Hot Dog and Other Poems* by Kit Wright, published by Kestrel Books 1981.)

    From Group Work (Intermediate) by Peter Watcyn-Jones © Penguin Books 2000